Truth

You Are The Distraction You Died Chasing

"You Were the Lie That Had to Die"

By

VIJAYA BHARATH REDDY ALLAVADA

Clever Fox® PUBLISHING

Chennai • Bangalore

CLEVER FOX PUBLISHING
Chennai, India

Published by CLEVER FOX PUBLISHING 2025

ISBN: 978-93-344-5647-9

Dedication

कालाय महाकालाय
सत्यस्वरूपाय नमः।

Salutations to Mahākāla
the
very embodiment of Truth.

PROLOGUE

Before You Begin

We begin with a hunger.
To know. To understand. To get to something final.
Something real.

Maybe you've carried that hunger for years.
Maybe it followed you into every room,
every silence, every moment that didn't quite answer what you hoped it would.

We all carry that ache.
Some call it curiosity.
Some call it spiritual seeking.
Some call it God.

But names don't matter here.
Not yet.

This is not a book of teachings.
There is no framework to memorize.
No practice to repeat.
No promise of bliss waiting on the last page.

This is a slow peeling.
Of words.
Of walls.
Of selves.

Each chapter is less about giving you something and more about taking something away.

If you came here to collect,
you may be disappointed.
If you came here to see,
then stay.

Read slowly.
Let the space between the lines do the work.

Let it unsettle you.
Let it ask what you never dared to ask.
Not about the world.
But about the **one watching it**.

Whatever you believe right now,
hold it gently.

Because what follows
may not give you more clarity.
But it may give you something better.

A stillness you didn't know you were running from.

Truth

You Are the Distraction You Died Chasing

But that truth won't shout.
It waits.
Just like it always has.

"निश्चल तत्वं शिवं उच्यते"

Nishchala tattvam Shivam uchyate

– *That which is unmoving… is called* ***Shiva****.*

PREFACE

They say truth is simple.
But when I looked at it, I found it hiding behind too many layers.

One day it looked like logic.
Another day, it danced like madness.
Sometimes it came with silence.
And sometimes it shouted like thunder.
And I stood there — asking: Which one is real?

So I began a journey.
Not outwards, but inwards.

I didn't go searching for answers in temples, books, or philosophies.
I just started watching... and listening.

I looked at my own thoughts.
At the sound inside my silence.
At how my eyes saw things and how something behind my eyes spoke without words.

I saw how truth isn't something you get.
It's something you grow into.
Not like a destination, but like a dance.This book is not a teaching.
It's a mirror.
For myself. And maybe, for you too.

Each chapter is not a step forward, but a deeper step in.
Into the way we look, the way we hear, and the way we create meaning around us.

We begin by exploring *what we see*,
then *what we hear*,
and eventually what we become.

We move from

My Lens to *Nothingness*.
From "I am that" to "I am not even that."
From chasing truth, to dancing with it.
From *Satyam*... to *Shivam*... to *Sundaram*.

Not as concepts.
But as felt truths.
Truths that can be touched with the voice inside us.

If you are holding this book,
you may already know that truth doesn't arrive with noise.
It whispers.
It stirs.

And if you're still enough, it shows you something:

That the world is not something you live in...
The world is something that lives in

you.

And so, we begin...

CONTENTS

GLOSSARY

A

Acharya *(aa-chaa-rya)* – A revered teacher or preceptor, especially in spiritual or scriptural matters.

Arjuna *(ar-joo-na)* – Central character in the Mahabharata; known for his unparalleled focus, archery skills, and devotion to dharma.

B

Bhagwan *(bhug-waan)* – A respectful term for God or a divine-like teacher.

Bhishma Pitamaha *(bheesh-ma pitaa-ma-ha)* – Grand-elder of the Kuru dynasty, a symbol of vow, duty, and sacrifice.

Brahmin *(braa-min)* – A member of the priestly class in Hindu society; often associated with knowledge and ritual.

C

Chitta *(chit-ta)* – The field of consciousness; the mind-stuff that stores impressions and memories.

D

Dakshina *(dak-shi-naa)* – A traditional offering or fee given to a guru or priest, often symbolic of gratitude and respect.

Dharma *(dhar-mah)* – The principle of cosmic order, righteousness, or moral duty.

Drupada *(dru-pa-da)* – A king in the Mahabharata; once a friend of Drona, later humiliated him.

Drona *(dro-na)* – Legendary teacher of archery and warfare in the Mahabharata; Guru to both Kauravas and Pandavas.

Duryodhana / Suyodhana *(dur-yo-dha-na / su-yo-dha-na)* – Eldest of the Kauravas; known for jealousy toward the Pandavas.

G

Guru *(gu-roo)* – A spiritual teacher or guide who removes darkness (ignorance) and leads one toward light (truth).

Guru Dakshina *(gu-roo dak-shi-naa)* – The offering a student makes to their guru at the end of learning.

K

Karma *(kar-ma)* – The law of cause and effect; actions and their resulting consequences.

Kauravas *(kau-ra-vas)* – The hundred sons of Dhritarashtra; rivals of the Pandavas in the Mahabharata.

Kunti *(kun-tee)* – Mother of the Pandavas, known for her wisdom and strength.

Kurukshetra *(koo-rook-she-tra)* – The battlefield of the Mahabharata war; symbolic of the inner battlefield of life.

Krupacharya *(kru-pa-chaa-rya)* – Royal teacher of Hastinapur and relative of Drona.

M

Mahākāla *(ma-haa-kaa-la)* – A fierce form of Shiva; the timeless and ultimate destroyer of illusion and ego.

Mahabharata *(ma-haa-bhaa-ra-ta)* – One of the two great Indian epics; a vast narrative of dharma, duty, and destiny.

Mantra *(man-traa)* – A sacred sound or phrase used in meditation or spiritual practice.

N

Nishchala Tattvam Shivam Uchyate *(nish-cha-la tatt-vam shi-vam uch-ya-te)* – "That which is unmoving is called Shiva"; highlights stillness as the essence of divinity.

P

Pandavas *(paan-da-vas)* – The five sons of Pandu: Yudhishthira, Bhima, Arjuna, Nakula, and Sahadeva.

Param Satya *(pa-ram sut-ya)* – The Absolute Truth; the highest, changeless reality.

Parashurama *(pa-ra-shu-raa-ma)* – The warrior-sage and teacher of Drona; sixth avatar of Vishnu known for his axe and spiritual wrath.

Pitamaha *(pi-taa-ma-ha)* – Grandfather; used with reverence for elders like Bhishma in the epic.

R

Roudrakarma *(row-dra-kar-ma)* – Symbolic name representing intense or fierce action.

S

Samādhi *(sa-maa-dhi)* – A deep meditative state where the sense of self dissolves; union with the object of meditation.

Sankalpa *(san-kal-pa)* – A solemn vow or mental resolve; intention behind action.

Satyam Shivam Sundaram *(sut-yam shi-vam sun-da-ram)* – "Truth, Godliness, Beauty" – a philosophical triad describing the ultimate reality.

Sutras *(soo-traas)* – Aphoristic texts or formulas conveying deep spiritual knowledge in condensed form.

Shunya / Mahā Shūnya *(shoon-ya / ma-haa shoon-ya)* – Zero or nothingness; in spiritual terms, the vast emptiness from which everything arises.

Shraddha *(shrad-dhaa)* – Reverent faith; the quiet, inner trust in one's path or teacher.

T

Turiya *(too-ree-ya)* – The "fourth" state of consciousness beyond waking, dreaming, and deep sleep; pure awareness.

V

Vajradut *(vaj-ra-doot)* – "Thunder-messenger"; name of a horse, suggesting speed and power.

Vedanta *(ve-daan-ta)* – A school of Indian philosophy exploring the nature of reality, consciousness, and the self.

CHAPTER 1

MY LENS, MY WORLD

How big is the world? Some say it's a small world. Others say it's vast beyond measure. But for most of us — for the common man,
the world is exactly the size of our lens.

Not the physical eye — but the inner one. The world starts at one corner of my lens and ends at another. Our world and our reality are merely that fraction which fits inside our lens. But what we see through our lens is just a tiny part of all that exits. Our view is limited by how we see things. We often think we understand everything around us, but what we see and understand is shaped by the point from which we are viewing and how we are trained to think.

It's important to think about how we see things and how our thoughts shape what we see. Our biases and what we've learned from school, society, and culture affect what we believe. And we should wonder if what we see is always the whole truth.

Imagine you're on a tall hill looking down. You see valleys, rivers, and distant towns. But when you come down to the valley, things look different. Mountains seem far, rivers look closer, and towns seem busier. Both views are true, but neither shows everything.

Truth is like a dance that changes with the music. When we change how we look at it, it changes too. Think about an Ant looking at the ground—it sees a flat surface. But we know from science that the Earth is round. And if you think about scientists studying space, to them, our Earth is just a small part of a huge group of stars called the Milky Way. So, truth looks different depending on how you see it.

To really know what's true, you should look at it from different angles. Different ways of looking show different colors and shapes of truth, just like a painter adding details to a painting. Our different ways of understanding are like different strokes of the brush adds something special to the painting, making it more interesting. Just like that, our different ways of seeing things add colors and details to what we know.

Different views add a touch to truth, but sometimes we get stuck on the surface. Imagine truth as a dance show where the dancers change their moves. We might focus on those changes, but what truly matters is the dancer—their feelings, thoughts, and the story they're telling with their dance.

Truth might seem different based on how we look at it, a bit like when we see the Earth from different spots. But it's not just about those changes in how truth looks. It's like the dancer behind the dance—there's something deeper that doesn't change. The main thing is to grab hold of the absolute truth. Underneath all those different views. Even if our way of seeing truth changes, the absolute truth —the thing that doesn't change—stays the same.

That absolute truth is also called Param[pa-ram] Satya[sut-yah]

Param Satya- परम सत्य .

Understanding absolute truth must happen in stages.

The first movement is the movement of seeing. This is the hardest part, not because truth hides, but because the mind has been trained for years to notice only fragments. It grabs a moment here, a thought there, a passing feeling — and believes that these small pieces are the whole picture. The mind reacts to whatever is closest, whatever is loudest, whatever feels urgent; it rarely senses the deeper current flowing underneath.

Learning to see beyond these scattered pieces — to feel the entire movement of life as one continuous flow — requires practice. It is like tuning an instrument that has been slightly off-key for a long time. You adjust it gently, patiently, again and again, until one day the sound becomes true. When the mind finally becomes still enough to hold the whole truth without breaking it apart, something ancient stirs within you — as if an old memory of who you really are comes alive for a moment.

The second movement begins on its own. It does not wait for your permission or effort. It is like an inner switch that turns on silently — an auto-start that no ritual can create and no force can stop. From this moment, understanding begins to unfold by itself, like fire moving through dry wood. You are no longer trying to understand truth; truth begins to understand *you*. It starts rearranging the structure of your seeing, your reactions, your clarity. Yet even this unfolding moves at its own pace, shaped by your honesty, your openness, and your inner readiness.

Then comes the third movement — the movement where everything becomes effortless. There is no pushing, no searching, no trying. Understanding becomes natural, like breathing, like sunlight slipping across a room. At this stage, you are not attempting to grasp the truth anymore; you have become transparent enough for truth to pass through you without resistance. Identity softens. Effort drops away. And when someone reaches this complete understanding of the absolute truth, they become part of it. Thoughts, beliefs, personality, identity, even karma begin to dissolve — not because something has taken them away, but because the one who held them is no longer separate.

Yet the truth is always there. We simply do not see it all at once. It is like looking at the sky through a narrow window. At first, you see just a bird crossing, a small patch of blue, or a drifting cloud. That little piece is real — but it is still only a fragment of the vastness beyond. The journey starts exactly like this: with a small seeing, a tiny glimpse that stirs something within. A thought, a feeling, a soft question rises from your depths — *Is there more?*

And so, you begin to look deeper. You practice. You sit quietly. You ask questions, not always with words, but with your heart. Slowly, the window becomes bigger. Now you can see the sky and the sun. You start to understand how things move, how shadows fall, how light returns.

This is the second stage — where you don't just see, but you start to understand what you are seeing. Not because someone tells you, but because something inside you knows.

Like when you understand a melody just by hearing it again and again — not with effort, but with attention.

And then, if you keep going, something beautiful happens. You stop needing the window at all. The walls disappear. There's no you looking at the sky anymore — there is only sky. You're not trying to understand the truth anymore... you are inside it. You are it.

At that point, you forget to ask questions. You forget your name, your thoughts, your opinions. Not in a sad way, but like how a wave forgets itself when it merges into the ocean.

That's the final stage: No more "me." No more looking. Only being.

So everything begins with seeing.

Not the casual kind we do every day — but a seeing that is sharp, focused, alive. A seeing that cuts through noise.
Before we explore, before we discover, before we even ask the right questions — we must see.
And seeing is not as easy as it sounds. It's not about using your eyes. It's about using your whole being.

To help you feel the depth of what I mean by "seeing," I want to take you into a moment you may already Understanding the absolute truth doesn't happen all at once. It unfolds — slowly, silently — in stages.

The first stage is often the hardest. It begins with *seeing*. Not just looking, but truly seeing — through all the noise, beyond distractions, into the heart of what is. This kind of seeing takes effort. Practice. A tuning of attention that doesn't happen overnight.

But once you get even a glimpse of that deeper truth — something shifts. The journey begins on its own. Like a seed touched by light, the process of understanding stirs to life without force.

In the beginning, that understanding is gentle and incomplete. You notice patterns. You make quiet connections. But full comprehension takes time — not just intelligence, but a certain ripeness of being. A readiness.

Then, as you stay with it, something beautiful starts to happen. You begin to flow with the truth rather than trying to chase it. Understanding becomes more natural, less effortful. Like a river finding its path.

And if you stay with the seeing — if you remain honest and open — there comes a moment where the process becomes fully automatic. You are no longer trying to understand the truth…
You dissolve into it.

Your thoughts, your beliefs, your identity — even your karma — begin to fall away.

Now, I know — that last part about karma might feel like a bold claim.
And it is.

But stay with me.
As we go deeper, we'll explore that too — patiently, honestly, and from many angles.

Now you might ask — what does this *seeing* really mean?

Let's bring it closer to life.

Truth is always there — but we rarely see it all at once.
It's like looking at the sky through a small window. At first, you only catch a piece — a bird passing, a patch of blue, maybe a cloud. That little glimpse is real. But it's only part of something much larger.

That's how the journey begins — with a small seeing. You sense something. A spark. A nudge. And a question arises from within:
"Is there more?"

So you begin to look deeper. You pause. You sit still. You ask — not always with words, but with your attention. Slowly, the window begins to widen. You see the sky stretch. You see the sun, the shifting clouds, the patterns of light and shadow.

This is where understanding deepens.

Not because someone explains it to you, but because something within you *recognizes* it.
Like how you understand a melody you've always known — not through effort, but through *attention*.

And then, if you stay with this awareness, something even more profound happens:
You forget the window entirely. The walls vanish.

There is no *you* looking at the sky anymore — there is only sky.

You are no longer trying to hold the truth.
You are held *inside* it.

Questions fade. The search ends.
Like a wave disappearing into the ocean — not lost, but returned.

That is the final stage.
No more seeking.
No more understanding.
Only *being*.

But for all of this to happen — everything must begin with seeing.

Not the casual kind we do every day. Not the seeing that's distracted or scattered.
I'm talking about a seeing that is *sharp*. Focused. Alive.

A seeing that cuts through the noise and lands right at the center of what matters.

Before we explore, before we analyze, before we name or define — we must learn how to *see.*

And to help you truly feel what I mean by this kind of seeing, I want to take you into a story.
One you may have heard before. But this time, let's not skim through it.

Let's slow down. Let's enter the story fully. Let's live it from within.

Let's go to the Mahabharata — and meet *Drona.*

Why Drona?

Because Drona is not just a teacher.
He is the embodiment of knowledge — of discipline, structure, and clarity.
He knows what is right. He carries the map.

But here's the quiet truth: knowing is not enough.

Drona holds wisdom like coal holds fire — *burning, but hidden.*
And at *this* stage in his life, that wisdom is wrapped in silence… and sometimes even sorrow.
The fire is still alive — but it's waiting.

What Drona needs now is someone who can *see* what he knows.
Not someone to praise him. Not someone to obey.
But someone to *recognize* the fire beneath the ash.
To draw it out. To reflect it. To make it real.

That someone… is *Arjuna*.

In this story, Drona is you.
And me. All of us.
All of us who carry truths inside us that we no longer know how to express.
Truths that once burned bright… but over time, became quiet.

And Arjuna — he is the part of us that awakens.
The part that still sees clearly. That acts decisively. That brings wisdom back to life.

We all carry a Drona within — the one who knows.
But until our inner Arjuna rises — the one who *sees* and *moves* — that knowing remains dormant.
Like fire beneath ash.

Even Drona, with all his knowledge, needed Arjuna's eyes to complete the lesson.
Just like we, too, often need someone — or some moment — to help us finally *see* what we already carry.

Because this story isn't just about archery.
It's about *seeing.*
And more importantly — it's about seeing only what matters.

Not about widening your view —
but narrowing it with purpose. Not about more light —
but about deeper focus.

So now… let's step into that ancient silence.
Let's watch what Drona asks.
Let's notice what Arjuna sees.

Here, we pause — to explore this moment from *Drona's* lens.

Because at this stage, Drona isn't the all-knowing master towering above his students.
He's more like any of us — full of insight, but covered in hesitation.
Like a flame waiting for wind.
A coal still warm, but not yet glowing.

When I looked at this moment through his eyes, everything slowed down.
The scene became sharper.
And suddenly, the story wasn't just about Arjuna's focus —
It was about Drona's longing…
To be *seen.*

And in that…
Isn't he all of us?

CHAPTER 2

EMBERS UNDER ASH

Before he stood as the fierce teacher of the Kauravas and the official guru of the kingdom, Drona was a humble Brahmin — learned in scriptures, skilled in warfare, but weighed down by poverty. His heart held the fire of knowledge, but his hands were empty. With a growing family and fading means, he was left with no choice but to seek help.

He wasn't chasing riches or power. All he longed for was a single cow — enough to feed his son. And so, with a hopeful heart, he turned to the one person he once called a true friend: Drupada, now a powerful king.

As boys, Drona and Drupada had been inseparable. They trained together, studied together, and shared dreams as equals. In those early days, Drupada had once promised with a wide grin, "When I become king, half my kingdom will be yours." Words spoken in youth — but words Drona never forgot.

Now, years later, worn by time and hardship, Drona arrived at the palace gates of Panchala with nothing but that memory in his heart and a quiet request on his lips.

But what met him inside those palace walls was not the warmth of friendship — it was a storm of humiliation.

Drupada did not rise to embrace him. He did not smile in recognition. Instead, the king looked at Drona as though he were a stranger — a beggar who had wandered too far. And with a voice sharpened by pride, he said:

"Friendship exists only between equals, Drona. You are no longer my equal."

The words cut deeper than any weapon.

Before a hall full of nobles, and with his wife and young son watching, Drona was not just denied — he was disgraced. Drupada dismissed their bond, rejected his plea, and ordered him to leave.

No war cry echoed that day. No thunder roared. But something broke inside Drona — silently, completely.

The pain didn't show on his face. It settled deeper, turning into something colder… something still. A vow that no one could hear — but one that would one day shape the fate of kings.

With nothing in hand and even less in heart, Drona walked away from the kingdom of Panchala. His pride shattered, his hope betrayed, he turned toward the only place left — the home of his in-laws in the neighboring kingdom of Hastinapur.

But the man who arrived in Hastinapur was no longer the same.

He had once come seeking help.
Now he carried a wound.
And that wound… would become his weapon.

After the humiliation in Drupada's court, Drona was a man walking through silence. His feet moved, but his spirit lagged far behind. He was heading toward his in-laws' home in Hastinapur — not because he wanted to, but because there was nowhere else to go. The fire of self-respect had burned out. His pride, once sharp and alive, now hung dull and silent like a broken sword.

He was minding his own path, lost in thought, when the sound of playful shouting reached his ears.

A group of young boys — princes, by the look of them — were playing with a ball near a large, ancient well. The ball had fallen in, and now they were all gathered around it, trying every way they could think of to get it out. Sticks. Ropes. Stones. Nothing worked. Their laughter was now tinged with frustration.

Drona noticed it, but said nothing. His instinct was to keep walking — not to interfere. His wounds were too fresh. His silence, too deep.

But then… something stopped him.

From the crowd of boys, one came running toward him.

He was lean and wiry, with dark skin that glowed under the sun. His eyes — half-closed, soft and sharp at once — reminded Drona of something ancient. Something divine. There was a calm power in those eyes, like Shiva in meditation. And when the boy smiled, it was like the moon had risen in daylight.

The boy ran up to Drona, folded his hands, and bowed deeply. Not out of habit — but reverence.

Then he touched Drona's feet.

"Bhagwan," the boy said gently, "we're in trouble. My brothers and I are trying to retrieve our ball from the well, but nothing is working. And just now, when I saw you walking by… you looked to me like Lord Shiva himself — traveling with Parvati and young Kartikeya."

He looked up, smiling. "None of my brothers saw you. Only I did. So I thought, maybe this is no coincidence. Maybe it's leela — divine play. You appeared without me doing any tapasya, and you seem to have come from far away… maybe even from Kailasa."

Drona just stood there.

He hadn't heard words like that in a long, long time.

Since the insult, no one had looked at him with respect. Not even his own reflection. The boy's voice, so innocent and full of wonder, felt like a stream of cold water touching a man lost in a desert.

Something in Drona's chest stirred — something he thought had died.

The boy's words didn't flatter him. They healed him.

In that moment, Drona did not feel like a failed father or a discarded friend. He felt seen. He felt remembered. Like the gods had whispered through this child, "You still have a place in this world."

A slow, warm smile spread across Drona's face — the kind of smile that hadn't come in years. It rose from the ashes of his pain and broke through the fog of his despair like sunlight after a storm.

He looked down at the boy and asked, his voice calm but glowing,
"Son… who are you?"

The boy's eyes were still bowed with respect, his hands folded in a gesture so natural it felt like it belonged to another world.

Then he spoke again — this time gently, but with the pride of one who carried great lineage without letting it weigh him down.

"Bhagwan," he said, with a smile that warmed the heart, "I am the middle son of Queen Kunti and King Pandu, younger brother of Yudhishthira and elder to Nakula and Sahadeva. My father is the late Pandu Raj — younger brother to Maharaj Dhritarashtra. The boys you see there — they are my brothers. The princes of Hastinapur."

There was no arrogance in his voice. Only the clarity of knowing who he was — and the reverence of knowing who stood before him.

He looked up again, his eyes full of something divine.

"Bhagwan… if you and Devi Mata would accept our humble *aathithi satkaar* — our offering of hospitality — it would be our honor. My grandfather, Bhishma Pitamaha, would be overjoyed to know that such a guest has come to our land. You appear weary. You've clearly walked a long way, barefoot and with great silence. Please… allow me to call for a chariot. Let us take you home and serve you, as one should serve a visiting god."

Drona stood still.

His face didn't change. Not yet. He was listening with his body, not his words. The boy's voice had a truth that no court had ever given him. This wasn't flattery. This was shraddha. Respect from a heart that knew no calculation.

And it pierced through something in Drona.

The part of him that had gone numb was beginning to stir again. Not as pride. Not yet. But as a breath.

A teacher's breath.

He didn't answer the boy's invitation. Not directly. Instead, he simply asked — quietly —
"What's the matter with the ball?"

The boy smiled. No offense taken.

He gently turned and led Drona toward the well.
"Come, Bhagwan," he said. "Let me show you."

As they walked together, the boy pointed toward his brothers one by one, introducing each with soft clarity and a familial twinkle in his voice.

"That is Yudhishthira, my elder brother — we call him Dharma Raj. He is the man of righteousness. Always calm, always fair."

Yudhishthira, noticing them, came forward and bowed with folded hands. Arjuna leaned closer and whispered something in his ear.

Dharma Raj nodded and turned to his younger brother.

"Arjuna," he said, "you have offered *aathithi satkaar* to this guest, and he has not yet spoken of acceptance. That itself is a teaching — but we must still act with dharma. Please, introduce him to our other brothers."

Then he turned to another young prince.

"Nakul," he said, "take your horse, Vajradut, and ride to Bhishma Pitamaha. Tell him: Arjuna, son of Pandu, has offered aathithi satkaar to a most noble guest. Request Pitamaha to come to our palace without delay. And go…" — he paused for just a breath — "with the speed of the wind."

Nakul bowed — eyes shining with purpose — and sprinted toward the stables without a word. Loyal as the wind, fast as a thought, he mounted Vajradut and vanished like a streak of lightning across the palace grounds.

Drona watched all this in silence.

Their movements were not rehearsed. Their words were not weighed. These were children — and yet they carried the spirit of kings.

And in the middle of it all stood Arjuna — dark, radiant, eyes half-closed like a young ascetic, yet full of youthful joy. The boy who saw him when no one else did. The boy who spoke to him like he was Shiva.

The boy who — with nothing but words — brought breath back to a broken teacher.

Drona did not speak.

But inside him, something shifted quietly.
The silence wasn't heavy anymore.
It had begun to listen.

Drona stood beside the well, now surrounded by all the boys — one hundred and five of them. The sons of Pandu and Dhritarashtra, gathered under the same sun, princes of the same bloodline, yet so different in spirit.

He glanced at them quietly, then asked — not as a teacher, but as a man testing the minds of the future:

"So… there are a hundred and five of you. And one lost ball. What is your solution?"

Bhima, tall and broad-shouldered, stepped forward confidently.

"If someone can go into the well," he said with pride, "I'll tie a rope to him and pull him out once he gets the ball. Easy."

Before Drona could respond, another boy stepped forward — this one radiant, proud, and dripping with strength. It was Suyodhana, son of Dhritarashtra. The first of the Kauravas.

"We are a hundred brothers," he said with a grin, "sons of Dhritarashtra. We can form a human chain and reach the bottom. And I can hold all of them with one hand."

There was laughter. Swagger. A sparkle of ego.

Then came a calm, thoughtful voice — it was Arjuna.

"Maybe there's another way," he said softly. "Without so much display of might. If we all hang over the well, the walls may collapse… and we'll lose the ball completely."

His words settled over the group like a quiet wind.

Drona's eyes turned toward him.

"Have you begun your training in archery yet?" he asked the group.

All of them nodded.

"Yes, we've started," said Bhima. "But how will bows and arrows help here?"

Arjuna raised his hand, ideas already forming.

"If we had a rope," he said, "I could tie it to an arrow and shoot toward the ball. It might stick or wrap around it... then we could pull it up."

Bhima chuckled.

"If we had a rope, I'd have tied Sahadeva to it and pulled both of them up by now."

The group burst into another round of laughter.

Suyodhana was about to say something — likely louder, possibly sharper — but before he could, Drona raised his hand.

A single gesture.
And the well went silent.

Then he spoke — voice calm, eyes steady:

"Might is a great tool. It can end battles. It can build kingdoms. But... it's not always the right solution."
He looked at each one of them.
"The world is moving toward precision — the intelligent use of power. Knowledge, not just strength, will shape the

future. In every field, it is not muscle… but technique that leads to true prosperity."

He turned to Arjuna.

"You said we could use an arrow and a rope. But what if… we don't have rope?"
His voice sharpened slightly, but with playfulness.
"What if… we use arrows in place of rope?" Arjuna's eyes widened.

The idea had never crossed his mind — but the moment he heard it, he could see it.

His heart leapt.

"Bagwan!" he said, hands joining in devotion, "I have heard tales of Shiva's bow — Pinaka Pani. But I have never seen it. I never even dreamed I would see the bowman himself."
He smiled with boyish hope.
"But today, I see you. And if luck blesses me, I may even witness Pinaka Pani in action."

Drona looked at him — really looked.

There was no flattery in Arjuna's words. No need to impress. Just reverence. Curiosity. Love for learning.

In that moment, something stirred in Drona's heart.
A small, still echo of the boy he once was.

The hunger to know. The joy of discovery. The humility to bow before greatness, not out of fear, but out of love.

For Drona, Arjuna became a mirror — of everything he once stood for… and everything he longed to pass on. From that day forward, the bond was forged.

Drona's love for Arjuna was born not out of favoritism — but recognition.
He saw not just a student… but a continuation of his own soul.
And that love… never faded.

The crowd of boys stood breathless.
All eyes were fixed on the man who hadn't claimed to be a teacher — but whose every movement now commanded the stillness of a forest just before the monsoon breaks.

Drona reached behind him and pulled out a simple bow — worn with time, but pulsing with presence. He placed his palm gently on its curve, closed his eyes, and whispered a sacred mantra under his breath.

The air shifted.

Even the princes — children of kings and gods — sensed something unusual. It was as if even the dust in the sunlight had paused to watch.

From his quiver, Drona drew eleven arrows.

He held ten between the fingers of both hands, arranged with such effortless grace that even the youngest among them could feel the power of control — not brute force.

The eleventh, he placed quietly beside him on the ground.

He stood tall, chest stretched, gaze level, eyes scanning the group of awestruck princes.

"We fire ten," he said, his voice calm and deep.
"But the first… is never meant to hit."

Arjuna tilted his head, puzzled.
"Why, Bhagwan?" he asked. "Why begin with a shot that's not meant to strike?"

Drona looked at him with a soft smile, then turned slightly toward the group, his fingers still steady on the string.

"Before you shoot an arrow at a target," he said, "just after the string is drawn and the body finds its stance — you fire one blank."

He looked at Arjuna as he spoke — not to teach, but to invite him into something sacred.

"It's not to hit. It's to bow."
"It's an offering. A salute. To your Guru, to the art, to the silence from which precision is born."

The boys stood still. Arjuna leaned slightly forward.

"But it's not just for reverence," Drona continued.
"The blank gives you information. It shows you the truth of your own body — the tension in your fingers, the drift in your breath, the alignment of your sight. It reveals what even you didn't know was off."

He paused, and the well beside him seemed to deepen with his words.

"But remember — the blank must never be fired at the actual target. That's the mistake of arrogance. If it misses — and it often will — it reveals your position to the enemy. Especially if you're hidden. A missed arrow is not just a waste… it's a warning to your opponent."

Arjuna's eyes sparked with deeper curiosity.
"Guruji, in a normal case, how does a student offer respect with the bow?"

Drona smiled.

"If the Guru permits," he said, "the student fires two arrows at the Guru's feet — they must land within half an inch of his toes, on either side, without touching."

The boys inhaled in disbelief.

"And just as the Guru looks down — that moment of instinct," Drona continued, "the disciple shoots two more arrows — grazing past the Guru's ears. The tail-feathers should brush them. Not cut. Not miss. Brush."

Arjuna stood silent — eyes wide, somewhere between reverence and disbelief.

"That," Drona said gently, "is real Guru Vandana. Not flowers. Not chants. Precision. Awareness. Total surrender."

And then, the world stilled again.

Drona turned toward the well.

He held the ten arrows delicately in his fingers — like verses of a sacred hymn waiting to be sung. But before he aimed, he raised his eyes to the sky — toward the sun, letting its rays fall on his brow.

And softly, with the tone of a disciple remembering his own teacher, he whispered:

"Hey Parashurama… Jai Gurudev."

Then, in one smooth breath, he fired the first blank arrow toward the southern sky — the direction of his Guru.

It flew with no aim but full intention — like incense disappearing into wind.

Then he turned to the well.

No commands. No announcement.

Only action.

His fingers moved.

Ten arrows flew.

But the boys didn't see ten arrows flying.
They heard one sound.

A deep, soft burst — as if the air itself had opened, gasped, and sealed again.

They rushed to the edge of the well — and what they saw would remain etched in their minds forever.

The ball, resting at the bottom of the dark well, had been pierced by one arrow.

But that arrow had another arrow locked into its tail.
And another.
And another.

All ten arrows had formed a chain — perfectly aligned, arrowhead into tail, spiraling downward like a golden vine suspended in air.

Not a single arrow missed.

Not a single angle faltered.

It wasn't just skill.

It was clarity, control, and devotion — all released in a breath.

Arjuna turned to Drona, his voice hushed by awe.

"Bhagwan…" he said. "I see now. The blank fire was not empty. It was everything."

He paused, his eyes steady and full of quiet light.

"And after that shot… something in you changed. Just a little. But I saw it."

Drona turned, surprised.
"What do you mean?"

Arjuna took a breath.

"You slowed your breathing… just a little — to adjust the stillness."
"You shifted your right foot — lowered it by a finger's width. To adjust the angle, maybe."
"Your chin dipped slightly — perhaps to see the target better from that posture."
"And your eyebrows… relaxed — maybe to sharpen your vision, to steady your gaze."
He paused.
"Maybe. I don't know. But I saw it."

Drona stared at him — stunned.

These weren't tricks he had taught. These weren't patterns any child could have guessed. These were reflexes born of years of inner alignment — unconscious movements of a seasoned master.

Yet this boy — this lean, soft-spoken prince — had noticed.

Not just the result.
Not just the arrows.

But the silence between the arrows.

And in that moment, Drona felt something shift in his heart.

Not pride.
Not relief.
But recognition.

This boy hadn't just witnessed a demonstration.

He had witnessed him.

And Drona knew — with no doubt:

This was the student.
The one who would carry his soul forward.
Not in blood, but in spirit.
Not in repetition, but in reflection.

And that bond… was now sealed.

The Bond Is Sealed – And the Kingdom Listens

The boys stared into the well, still stunned by the sight of the ten arrows spiraling down like a divine staircase, the ball pierced cleanly at the center.

But before they could absorb the moment, Bhima stepped forward, his excitement overflowing.

"I'll bring it up!" he shouted, leaping forward with his usual fire.

Suyodhana, not to be left behind, charged toward the well from the other side.

The two collided at the edge — Bhima's shoulder hitting Suyodhana's chest with force.

Suyodhana, caught off-balance, stumbled and fell to the ground. There was a gasp among the boys — but Bhima didn't even notice. He reached down, pulled the ball out from the cluster of arrows, and held it up like a trophy.

Without pride or mockery, he turned to Yudhishthira, Dharma Raj, and gently handed it over.

Yudhishthira took it with a quiet nod, then walked over to the fallen Suyodhana — and placed the ball in his hands.

No words.
Just dignity.
Even in rivalry, Dharma was to be followed.

Before any more could be said… the ground seemed to respond to the sound of approaching hooves and wheels.

A royal chariot came into view, golden banners fluttering in the wind.

The boys turned in unison.
They knew that presence.
That poise.
That silence.

Bhishma Pitamaha had arrived.

Everyone bowed.

Even the wind seemed to pause to offer its salute.

Bhishma stepped down from the chariot, his long white beard swaying gently, his armor catching the sunlight like a prayer in metal. He walked straight toward Drona with folded hands and a warm smile.

“My respects, O noble Brahmin,” he said. “I am Bhishma — the humble servant of my Guru, Parashurama.”

The boys gasped.

“Bagwan’s Guru too is Parashurama Dev!” one of them said aloud.

Drona bowed in return, his face softening for the first time in days.

Bhishma gestured toward the young boy beside Drona.

"This child… Ashwatthama, I believe?"

Drona nodded.

"He looks hungry," Bhishma said gently, with the care of a grandfather.

"Sahadeva," he called out, "run to the chariot. The silver vessel that Nakula holds — bring a glass of milk for the boy."

Sahadeva nodded and rushed. From Nakula's hands, he took a silver tumbler, dipped it into the brass pot resting in the chariot, and brought back a warm glass of milk, holding it as if carrying something sacred.

He placed it in Ashwatthama's hands with a smile.

Drona watched this with eyes glistening.
Respect.
Kindness.
Grace.

He hadn't expected this. He had only walked into Hastinapur to rest. Now… he was being welcomed like a Rishi.

Drona looked up, surprised. "My father-in-law lives in the city," Drona said. "His name is Kripacharya.

"Krupacharya?" Bhishma repeated.
"The royal teacher?"

Bhima smiled.

"Yes. He teaches us all. And he will be delighted to know his own samdhi is here."

Bhima gently took Drona's arm.

"Please… come. Eat. Rest."

Drona didn't resist.

He was tired — not in body, but in soul. And the kindness around him was not something he could ignore.

At the palace, a meal was laid out. Simple. Warm. Made with love.

Drona ate in silence, Ashwatthama beside him. For the first time in many days, his son had milk in his hands and food in his belly.

After the meal, Bhima bowed once more.

"You have come as a guest, Guruji," he said, "but to us, you already feel like family. Please rest tonight — and tomorrow, if you must go, we will not stop you. But let this day end with peace."

Drona smiled and nodded. The fatigue in his bones was heavier than he admitted.

He slept that night — not in gold, not in comfort — but in dignity.

The morning sun had barely crossed the palace walls when Bhishma Pitamaha arrived again — this time not with soldiers or fanfare, but with quiet intent in his heart.

Drona, still preparing to leave, turned as the Grand Sire entered with his gentle yet commanding presence.

Bhishma bowed slightly — not out of formality, but with deep respect.

"Acharya Drona," he said, "I've heard of yesterday's events from the children."

He stepped forward, eyes calm but glowing with meaning.

"And I must tell you something quite rare — all the princes, Pandavas and Kauravas alike, speak of you with one voice."

Drona looked down, uncomfortable with such open praise.

Bhishma continued:

"Children who argue over everything… agreed on you."
"They were not merely impressed by what you did — they were changed by it."

He placed a hand gently over his chest.

"And as the protector of this kingdom and the architect of its future, it is my duty to prepare these young minds — not just with weapons, but with values."

He looked Drona in the eye.

"If you would show mercy upon Hastinapur… and become its Royal Guru, you would not just serve this land — you would shape its very destiny."

Drona was silent.

He had not come for this. He had already received more than his bruised pride had ever hoped for — food, shelter, respect, love.

He opened his mouth to humbly refuse.

"Pitamaha… I am honored beyond words. I never came here with expectations. Your kindness is already more than I—"

But Bhishma raised his hand, and with a firm, fatherly smile, interrupted him.

"You are the Parashurama of this generation, Acharya."
"And every generation needs a Parashurama."

At that name — his Guru's name — Drona paused.

It wasn't praise that stopped him. It was truth.

In that moment, he remembered the voice of his own teacher, the weight of his bow, the scent of old forests where he once trained… and the fire that had once lived in his own heart.

He bowed deeply.

"If it is the will of the kingdom…" he said, "then this Brahmin will serve."

Preparations began that very day. The city of Hastinapur shimmered in celebration. From the palace balconies to the temple bells, the entire kingdom turned its eyes to a single ceremony — the appointment of Acharya Drona as the Royal Guru of the House of Kuru.

Golden chariots lined the palace steps. White canopies were raised. Priests chanted Vedic hymns in unison as Drona was led into the court.

The crown gifted him:

Hundreds of cows, their horns painted, garlanded in lotuses.

Chests of gold, silver, gems, and silken robes.

A vast estate of farmland to sustain his household for generations.

A home within the royal compound, built in sandalwood and marble.

And most of all — a royal scroll, naming him Rajaguru of Hastinapur, with full signature authority in the education of princes.

But amidst all the grandeur, Drona's eyes searched only for one face.

Arjuna.

And there he was — the first to reach him, before the others.

He ran through the ceremonial crowd, breathless with joy, and fell at Drona's feet.

Drona gently placed a hand on his head.

"What do you seek, Arjuna?"

The boy looked up — eyes gleaming, voice steady:

"I want to become like you, Gurudev."
"An archer. The best of the best. Just like you."

Drona smiled — but in his heart, he whispered:

"Not just like me, Arjuna… but someone who will one day surpass me."

At the final moment of the ceremony, Bhishma stepped forward with a silver bowl filled with sacred water from the Ganga.

He held Drona's hand over the fire.

And Drona declared, his voice rising like thunder woven in silk:

"From this day forth, I, Drona — son of Bharadwaja, disciple of Parashurama — offer my body, mind, and skill to Hastinapur."

"I shall train its princes with fairness and fire."
"I shall protect its honor with wisdom and warcraft."
"And I shall stand by the crown... no matter what storms may come."

The crowd thundered:

"Jai Acharya Drona!"
"Jai Rajaguru!"

And thus, a teacher became more than a mentor.

He became an arm of the kingdom.

And at his side... stood a boy whose arrows would one day shake the world.

CHAPTER 3

THE BOW WAITED, THE ARROW KNEW

The ceremonial dust had barely settled. The chants from Drona's appointment as Rajaguru still lingered in the marble corridors. But Drona's mind was already elsewhere — not on celebration, but on preparation.

One morning, Drona approached Bhishma Pitamaha, who stood watching the palace gardens with hands folded behind his back.

"Pitamaha," Drona said respectfully, "the time has come for me to begin training these princes."

Bhishma nodded.

"We are all eager for your guidance, Acharya."

But Drona paused, then added with quiet concern:

"Before we begin, I must speak plainly. There are already two clear factions among these children — a group that follows Suyodhana, and one that stands around Yudhishthira and his brothers. The Kauravas — a hundred of them — versus the five sons of Pandu."

Bhishma turned to him, expression serious.

"Yes. I have seen the tension. But do you think it will affect their training?"

Drona exhaled.

"That is exactly my concern. If I train them all within the palace, among comforts, politics, and distractions — they will never learn as one body. There will always be whispers, rivalries, and the weight of courtly eyes."

He looked into the distance.

"I wish to take them away. To a forest. A training camp. A sacred grove — free from noise. Let them sweat, stumble, and grow in solitude. Let the arrows fly into trees before they fly into each other."

Bhishma thought for a long moment.

"Can there be no other way?"

"I have considered every path," Drona replied gently. "And this, I believe, is the cleanest one. If you trust me, Pitamaha... I ask for this."

Bhishma placed a hand on his shoulder.

"Then it shall be done."

Gurugraha: The Forest of Discipline

And so, Bhishma made arrangements.

Within days, a camp was constructed on the edge of the forest — a serene place surrounded by woods and still waters. The site was named Gurugraha — "The Teacher's Abode."

Simple huts were built. Open grounds cleared. A sacred fire lit. This was not a palace. This was a cradle for warriors.

And here, the 105 princes of Hastinapur arrived — dressed not in royal silks, but in plain robes, carrying only the essentials.

It was here, far from the throne, that their real journey would begin.

Drona's first command surprised them.

"There will be no weapons in the first week," he said.
"Only silence."

He asked them all to wake at 5 a.m. sharp, and after bathing in the river, sit in meditation.

Their first exercise?

"Close your eyes," he instructed, "and hold the image of a glowing flame in your mind — a small oil lamp. See it. Feel it. Hold it steady without letting the flame flicker. Do this every day."

At first, most of the boys struggled. Some grew restless. Others dozed off. A few whispered and giggled.

But Arjuna sat like stone.

Day after day, he sat in stillness, sweat running down his back, his spine upright, his gaze inward — holding that image of the flame without letting it shake.

Drona watched silently from a distance. He said nothing. But he saw.

Then came the next exercise.

"Now," Drona said, "look at the sky without blinking. Fix your gaze on a single point — a star, a leaf, a mark in the clouds. Hold it. Do not flinch."

Again, Arjuna excelled.

His eyes did not flutter. His mind did not wander. His attention cut through space like an arrow not yet released.

Drona noted it all.

"He's already aligning," he thought.
"Before I even touch the bow."

The day before their training began, Drona gathered all 105 students near the sacred banyan at Gurugraha. The camp buzzed with youthful energy. But Drona's presence hushed it like twilight silencing birdsong.

He stood before them, hands behind his back, eyes scanning each face.

"Tomorrow," he said, "we begin your training. Each of you must choose your primary weapon and the form of combat you wish to master. Sword, mace, spear, or bow — all are noble."

He paused.

"But," he continued, "regardless of your choice, I expect every one of you to learn archery as your secondary art. If not your primary. One skilled archer… can change the fate of an entire army."

There was silence, but not confusion. The boys nodded. They could feel the gravity of his words.

The Principles of War

Drona stood before the gathered princes, his voice calm but edged with the weight of many battles.

"The first principle is strength — to overpower the enemy with sheer might. This is the most direct path. It is the base of any battlefield."

He paused, letting the truth of it settle.

"But strength alone is not enough. If your enemy is as strong as you — or stronger — then strength becomes limited. It's time-consuming to grow, and sometimes… you don't have time."

The boys listened, attentive. Arjuna sat straight, Bheema slightly impatient. But it was Yudhishthira, ever the thinker, who leaned in when Drona said:

"In such cases, we turn to strategy."

He began pacing slowly in front of them.

"Formations. Timing. Position. Speed. Distance. Wealth."

Yudhishthira raised his hand gently, a flicker of curiosity in his eyes.

"Guruji, how do we use things like time… or wealth… in battle?"

Drona stopped. A good question. He turned to face the princes fully, his voice dropping slightly — as if he was about to reveal something ancient, almost mystical.

"When facing a stronger enemy," he said slowly, "study his timeline."

He reached for a scroll, unrolling it on the ground.

"Look at his nakshatra. His grahas — his planetary influences. Not because we believe the stars control our fates like puppets... but because they tell a story."

The air stilled. Even Bheema looked confused.

Drona continued.

"You see, in the old ways — priests would say: Don't march during the waning moon. Never strike under the shadow of Moola nakshatra. They would chant mantras to Mars, to Saturn, to Rahu. Superstition, they called it. But what were they really doing?"

He tapped the scroll gently.

"They were watching patterns. Emotional tides. Days of grief. Days of pride. Days when a man lets his guard down — not because the stars command it, but because men are men. They celebrate. They mourn. They forget. That's what a horoscope tells you — not destiny… but distraction."

The young princes were silent now, not in confusion — but in dawning comprehension.

Drona's eyes met Yudhishthira's.

"Know your enemy this well," he said, "and you'll know exactly when to strike."

Yudhishthira sat back, breath caught halfway.

"So it's not astrology," he murmured. "It's awareness."

Drona smiled faintly.

"Exactly," he said. "And that… is the difference between superstition — and strategy."

Drona continued.

"Next… is wealth," he said, his voice sharpening into something colder.

"An army burns gold as fast as it draws blood."

He paused, letting the words settle like a blade on skin.

"Every soldier you see — every sword that swings, every horse that gallops, every wound that bleeds — consumes wealth. Food, water, weapons, tents, armor, medicines, messengers, spies, bribes... war doesn't run on valor. It runs on coin."

He walked slowly along the sanded courtyard, gaze fixed, voice low and lethal.

"The mightier the force, the more it must eat. The more it must feed. The more it must be stitched, armed, replaced, and kept alive for the next kill."

"You don't have to face such a force head-on," he continued, eyes narrowing.
"You bleed it from within. Not by the sword. But by the purse."

"If you can choke its gold," Drona said with quiet brutality, "you won't need to spill its blood. The army will collapse — not from wounds, but from hunger."

"Starve the treasury, and the soldiers will starve themselves. That… is strategy."

He turned, his eyes narrowing.

"Your sword need not touch their general. Just choke his treasury. Bleed his coin. Let the horses go hungry. Let the metal rust for lack of oil. Let the soldiers break formation for want of pay. That is how armies fall — not always with a roar, but with a slow, quiet decay."

He paused, letting that sink into the bones of every boy sitting there.

Then — colder now:

"Delay the war."

"Drag them into monsoon. Let the skies do what your arrows cannot."

"Force their chariots into the mud. Let their wheels drown in slush. Let their boots rot. Let them sleep in wet tents, wake to snake bites, and curse the rain more than your name."

"Attack their stables at night. Slaughter the elephants before the war begins. Burn their fodder. Poison their wells. Release venomous snakes into their drinking jars."

The boys were frozen — eyes wide, breath held — unsure whether they were listening to a warrior… or a shadow.

"Make them build," Drona continued.
"Force them to defend. Let them waste time building walls, not launching arrows. Turn every step into a struggle. Let the mud, the wind, the sickness, and the silence wear them down."

"Even gods," he said, his voice dry and bitter, "will lose morale if their horses are starving."

He stood still, then spoke the final truth — sharp as poison.

"And lastly — fear."

"Send spies. Poison few men, quietly. Make it look divine. Let a whisper spread: 'A curse has begun.' 'The stars have turned.' 'The river goddess is angry.'

He smiled without warmth.

"Stories can split an army before any blade is drawn. Doubt spreads faster than fire. Morale is the spine of any force — snap it, and they collapse into each other."

Then Drona grew still.

The firelight flickered on his face — not warming it, but revealing the iron beneath.

"But," he said, turning to each of them, "none of this matters… if you don't know how to fight."

"Your weapon is not a tool. It is not your servant. It is your breath. Your limb. Your thought. You must become so close to it, it moves before you speak. Not like a sword… but like a shadow."

He looked at Arjuna then — the boy didn't move, but something in him listened more sharply than the others.

The Sun and the Flame

Drona looked at the sky.

"Tomorrow," he said, "you'll begin weapon training. But before that — we train the *eye*."

" Before anything else — we train the eye."

He took a breath, as if reciting an ancient truth etched in fire.

"नेत्रं मूलं विजयानां। नेत्रेण युद्धं प्रारभ्यते, मनसा जयः निष्पद्यते।"

(*Netraṁ mūlaṁ vijayānām. Netreṇa yuddhaṁ prārabhyate, manasā jayaḥ niṣpadyate.*)

"The eye is the root of victory. Battle begins with the eye; victory is completed by the mind."

The boys fell silent. A sacred kind of silence.

"Every morning, before the sun rises — complete your meditation. Sit still. Breathe. Empty your mind like a calm lake."

"Then, as the sun crests the horizon, stare at it."

He pointed east, already imagining the golden rise.

"Do not flinch. Do not blink. Let the light strike your skin. Let it burn your forearms. Let your eyes water. Stay."

"This is how you learn stillness."

"This is how your body learns to obey your will."

And the next day — they did.

All 105 boys sat in rows in the damp hush of dawn, wrapped in silence. As the first golden fireball broke through the sky, they turned east and fixed their gaze.

The light grew. The wind cooled. The pain built slowly, quietly — like fire wrapping around their arms and faces. Eyes stung. Knees trembled. Sweat rolled down necks. But still — they stayed.

And among them, one boy did not blink once.

Arjuna.

Not because he had no pain...
...but because he had already forgotten what pain was.

His body had ceased to resist. His eyes had stopped negotiating.
Only his breath remained — steady, sharp, and surrendered.

Guru Purnima: The Day of Offering

The following day was Guru Purnima — the full moon dedicated to the teacher, the flame through which knowledge passed from generation to generation.

The air that morning was gentler. Even the birds seemed to fly slower.

The boys rose early, bathed in the river, and dressed in clean white cotton.
The ashrama was alive — not with weapons or drills, but with flowers, grains, incense, and laughter. No orders. No marches. Only purpose.

Bheema was placed in charge of the kitchen — a decision that delighted him far more than any war exercise. He supervised the boiling of milk and roasting of grains with more seriousness than he showed on the battlefield.

"Don't stir too fast," he warned Nakula, "you'll bruise the rice."

Meanwhile, Suyodhana and Yudhishthira assisted Drona personally — carving a Pratima (sacred idol) of Parashurama, the axe-wielding sage who had once taught Drona himself. The wood was dense and heavy. Drona did not ask for help, but the boys brought tools and stood silently beside him, offering hands when needed.

At the far end of the courtyard, a group of younger boys sat cross-legged, gently molding small Shiva Lingas out of river clay — adorning them with turmeric, ash, and wildflowers plucked from the banks.

Ashwatthama, Drona's son, polished a small copper trident with careful precision. He said nothing, but his eyes rarely left his father.

By the time the sun had risen to their chins, all preparations were complete.

Each offering had its own place.
Shiva's altar was austere — a linga on a flat black stone, decorated with bilva leaves and silence. The boys had placed fruits and sweets beside it, but something about its simplicity made even the crows stay away.

But for Parashurama, the scene was different.

There were rows of dishes — carefully arranged by grain, spice, and sweetness. Clay pots filled with ghee and jaggery, plates of sesame ladoos, soft rice cakes, and even roasted yams. Drona's usually stern eyes softened for a moment as he looked at the offering. He didn't speak. He just bowed his head.

And then came Bheema, spoon in hand.

As usual, he tasted everything first — more out of hunger than ritual.

"Offerings must be tested," he mumbled through a mouthful of rice,
"or the gods might get indigestion."

The boys burst into laughter. Even Drona allowed a small smile.

But the moment didn't last.

A bell rang from the northern end of the courtyard.
It was time for the Guru-Dakshina — the sacred offering of gratitude from student to teacher.

One by one, each prince stepped forward with a simple gesture — a folded cloth, a handmade item, a verse of gratitude recited with folded hands. No gold. No jewels. Only effort and sincerity.

Then came Arjuna.

He stepped forward not with a gift in hand, but with a bow across his back.

And instead of speaking, he knelt — not to Drona, but before the idol of Parashurama — and touched his head to the ground. Then, rising slowly, he turned and placed the bow at Drona's feet.

"I offer this not as a weapon," he said quietly, "but as a promise."

Drona looked at the boy. Then at the bow. Then again at the boy.

No words were spoken. But something was sealed that day — not just between guru and student, but between destiny and discipline.

The Bird's Eye

After the pooja, Drona stood, his hand on the statue of Parashurama.

"Now," he said, "we begin."

He pulled out a wooden bird, carefully carved, and called Roudrakarma, one of the youngest students.

Roudrakarma ran forward, beaming.

Drona handed him the bird.

The boy's eyes sparkled.
"For me, Guruji?" he asked, clutching the bird like he'd just been named heir to the throne.

A ripple of chuckles passed through the group. Even the usually still Ashwatthama rolled his eyes.

Drona gave him a long, slow look — the kind that removed all illusion without raising its voice.

He raised one eyebrow.

"Yes, of course," he said dryly,
"a finely carved wooden bird, in the middle of a war school, during a weapons training announcement — clearly a gift."

The group laughed louder now.

Drona's smirk sharpened just slightly.

"Early celebrations," he added, stepping closer,
"often backfire. Sometimes what you think is a reward…"
He tapped the bird.
"…is nothing more than a beautifully disguised burden."

The boy blinked, confused.

Drona handed it to him anyway.

"Climb the tree," he said. "Tie it high. Make it sway."
"Let's see how many 'gifts' come flying at it today."

Roudrakarma nodded and did so.

Once the wooden bird swayed gently on the tree, Drona turned serious.

"Now listen."

His tone sliced through the warm air — firm, cold, deliberate.

"Most of the time, the arrow reaches where your sight reaches."

He drew a straight line in the dust with the tip of his staff.

Then, softly, like a whisper too dangerous to raise:

"दृष्टिर् एव मन्त्रः। यत्र दृष्टिः, तत्र सिद्धिः।"

(Dṛṣṭir eva mantraḥ. Yatra dṛṣṭiḥ, tatra siddhiḥ.)
"Gaze itself is a mantra. Where the gaze rests, success follows."

He didn't explain.

He didn't need to.

The boys had already stilled.

The wind shifted slightly, brushing their cheeks like an omen.
Drona continued — not with kindness, but with exactness.

"The moment your focus is absolute…"
He let the sentence drift, unfinished — as if the rest had to be found in silence.

Then his command came — short, final, without softness:

"Sit. Take aim. At the eye of the bird."

No mention of arms. No tips on wind or form.
No help.

Just the command — and the task.

Each boy took position.
One line. One target.

The wooden bird swung gently on the high branch, caught in a whispering breeze. Its painted eye blinked in the sun — a challenge hanging in the air.

They set their stances. Fixed their bows.
Breathed.

Each gaze lifted toward the tree, toward the tiny eye — as if the rest of the world had vanished.

Sunlight crossed their faces, now slightly past its peak — warm but distant. Time had thinned.

Then Drona began.
Slowly. Quietly. One name at a time.

"Bheema."

Bheema grinned like he was being crowned king.

"Guru Dev, I see… everything!
You, the tree, the bird, the Shiva Lingam, Parashurama's pratima, the camp… and the food! Especially the food! In different vessels!"

A wave of laughter passed through the group.

Drona smiled faintly.
"Absolutely. Now go enjoy that food you just mentioned."

Bheema practically leapt toward the lunch tents.

"Suyodhana."

He stepped forward with dramatic confidence.

"Everything Bheema saw! And…"
He leaned in, eyes twinkling,

"...I also see the food disappearing into Bheema faster than arrows in battle."

The courtyard erupted.

Drona sighed.
"A true warrior sees fast. But you're seeing too far. Go eat before Bheema finishes *your* portion too."

Suyodhana bowed theatrically and strolled off, grinning.

"Vikarna."

Always eager, always philosophical.

"Guruji, I see the bird… and the emptiness behind it. The stillness. The breath between the breath."

Drona stared at him.

"And yet you missed the eye. Go contemplate that… over lunch."

"Durmukha."

Full of drama. Too full.

"I see the bird, yes, but I also see fate. The arc of karma. The cycle of rebirth—"

Drona cut in.

"And I see indigestion if you don't stop talking. Go."

“Yuyutsu.”

Quiet. Sincere.

“I see a test, Guruji. Not just in the bird, but in us — in how we respond.”

Drona nodded slowly.
“A good mind. But right now, I need eyes, not essays. Go eat.”

“Durjaya.”

Puffed up with pride.

“I see the curve of the feathers, the grain of the wood, and the pattern of the shadows.”

Drona blinked.

“Very impressive. But it’s not art class. Go.”

“Ashwatthama.”

Drona’s own son.

He didn’t flinch. He didn’t hesitate.

“I see the mistake everyone else is making.”

A few boys turned their heads.

Drona didn’t comment. Just gave a nod.

“Eat. Then return. We’ll talk.”

"Shalya."

Ever the showman.

"I see a challenge placed in plain sight — but meant for only one archer."

Drona said nothing for a moment.
Then simply:
"You're not wrong. Go."

Student after student.
Answer after answer.

Poetry, pride, jokes, riddles — all fired off like stray arrows.

And each time, Drona listened.
Smirked. Or sighed.
Then sent them to lunch.

Until only one remained.

The wind had settled.

The laughter had faded.

And Drona finally said,
"Arjuna."

The Moment That Froze Time

The training ground was empty now.

Empty except for two figures.

Arjuna.
Drona.

The others had been dismissed, their arrows packed, their bows lowered. But this… this wasn't over.

This was no longer a simple lesson.

It was something else.

A ritual.
A recognition.
A revelation unfolding in real time.

Drona stood quietly for a moment, then spoke — his voice stripped of performance, steady as a blade drawn for truth.

"What do you see?"

A pause.

Arjuna's body didn't shift.
His head didn't tilt.
Only his lips moved — barely.

"The eye of the bird, Guru Dev."

His voice was soft. Too soft for a battlefield.
And yet, it sliced through the air like thunder.

Drona's head tilted, just slightly.

"What else?"

Another pause.
Then came the reply.

"Nothing else, Guru Dev."

The breeze passed like a whisper through the trees.
The leaves rustled, but Arjuna… did not.

Drona's eyes sharpened.

He stepped closer. His voice dipped lower — intimate, testing.

"Do you see me?"

"No, Guru Dev."

"Your brothers?"

"No."

"The tree?"

"No."

"The branch? The wings? The tail? The bird itself?"

"No… no… no… no."

Each "no" was softer than the last — but clearer than wind.

Each reply stripped away the world like peeling bark from a tree.

Until nothing remained.

Nothing but a line between gaze and target.

A bow.
An arrow.
A breath.

And a silence so deep, it no longer felt human.

Drona didn't say a word.

He stepped back. Slowly. Quietly.

His sandals barely stirred the dust.

He looked at Arjuna — not as a teacher now, but as a man who had just uncovered a hidden fire.

Then... Drona walked toward the tree.

The same tree the wooden bird swung from.

And without explanation...
He sat down.

Right beneath it.
A few feet from Arjuna.

Facing him.
Facing the arrow.
Facing what was unfolding.

He crossed his legs and placed his staff beside him.

He did not speak.

He just… watched.

Arjuna stood motionless.

Not breathing — or barely breathing.

His stillness wasn't discipline anymore.
It was possession.

As if some ancient force had claimed him — rooted him to the earth.

He was not a boy.
He was not even a warrior yet.

He was aim itself.

Minutes passed.

And more.

The world moved on.

From the tents nearby came the sound of spoons clanging against metal.

The scent of ghee and rice and sweet jaggery drifted on the breeze.
The laughter of boys at lunch — full, loud, careless.

And yet — across the courtyard…

Time had stopped.

Drona and Arjuna sat opposite each other,
locked in a silence that now felt… divine.

One by one, the students began to return.

Not out of duty. Not because they were called.

Because they sensed something.

Curiosity at first.

Then confusion.

Then awe.

They stopped at the edge of the yard.

Saw Drona seated like a monk.
Saw Arjuna — frozen in eternal aim.

Not wavering. Not blinking. Not even trembling.

And something shifted inside each boy.

The ones who had joked before —
Now stood still, goosebumps rising across their skin.

It was as if they had walked in on a secret…
too sacred to speak of.

Bhima, now full from lunch, felt his chest swell.

Not with laughter.
But with something deeper. Older.
Pride.
Pride that hurt the throat when held in.

"That's *my* brother," he whispered to himself.

But Suyodhana…

His palms were sweating.

His lips had gone dry.

He watched the arrow. Then the eye. Then the stillness.

And a single thought rose in his mind like poison:

"This one… will haunt me forever."

He could feel it.

Like the shadow of a nightmare that hadn't come yet…
but was already waiting.

The other Kauravas stared — transfixed, frightened.

As if they were watching their own end written in the still air.

Drona, seated beneath the tree, finally stirred.

He turned to Yudhishthira, who had silently joined the group.

A soft nod.

"Keep watching," Drona whispered.

Then — without a word to Arjuna — he rose and walked away.

He washed his hands.
Sat.
Ate his simple meal — rice and curd.
No spices. No sweets.
Nothing to distract him from the taste of what he had just witnessed.

Then he lay down. Closed his eyes. Slept.

And the camp — held its breath.

No shouting.
No whispering.
Not even the birds dared.

An hour passed.

Drona awoke.

He walked to the river.

Bathed.
Performed his Sandhya Vandana — facing the setting sun with folded hands.

And then…
He returned to the training ground.

Arjuna hadn't moved.

Not one finger.
Not one breath louder than before.

And now — every student had returned.

They stood behind the Guru, forming a silent circle around the boy.

They didn't speak.
They didn't blink.
They didn't even look at each other.

Because everything — everything — was happening inside that moment.

Inside that one arrow.

Inside that one gaze.

Even the birds in the tree had fallen still.

As if they, too, were afraid to flap their wings —
lest they distract the only boy in the world

who was no longer in the world.

Drona stepped forward.
The silence around him held its breath.
The boys stood frozen behind him.
The air... heavier than before.

He walked slowly, step by step, until he stood once again just a few feet away from Arjuna — whose bow was still drawn, his gaze still locked.

And then — with the gentleness of a secret being told only to the soul —

Drona whispered:

"Arjuna..."

No response.

Not a blink.
Not a shift.

Just the faintest breath escaping from Arjuna's nose —

as if the body had momentarily forgotten it was alive.

Then, from somewhere deep inside that statue of stillness...

"Hmmmm..."
A soft hum. Like the end of a dream. Or the beginning of one.

Drona leaned in closer.
"Arjuna."

This time, even softer.
A breath, more than a word.

"Ummmmm…"
Arjuna's lips barely moved. His voice wasn't speaking — it was *echoing* from some cave inside him.

Drona's voice grew just a shade louder — enough to stir a ripple in the fabric of silence.

"Arjuna."

That name, again. Like a bell.

And this time…

Arjuna moved.

Not his limbs.
Not his posture.
Just his voice.

A steady, grounded whisper — like he was waking from a deep samādhi,
not startled… but called.

"Gurudev."

Drona's eyes flickered — the moment had returned.

He asked, still low:

"Is the bird moving?"

A pause.

Arjuna's brow twitched — the first motion in hours.

"I don't think so, Guru Dev."

The words came slow, careful. As if he was trying not to disturb the line between himself and the eye.

Now — even the trees were listening.
Not a bird chirped. Not a leaf stirred.
Everything waited.

"What do you see?"

Arjuna didn't blink.

His answer didn't come quickly.
It came *completely*.

"The bird's eye, Guru Dev."

"The branch?"
"No."

"The tree?"
"No."

"Me?"

"No."

"Your brothers?"
"No."

"The bird?"
"No."

"Just the eye?"
"Just the eye."

Drona's voice dropped lower.

Softer than the breeze.
Quieter than the rustling leaves.
But heavier than stone.

He took a slow step closer, still standing between Arjuna and the setting sun.

His eyes narrowed with curiosity — not doubt, but *wonder*.

"Arjuna…"
"Are you hungry?"

A strange question. At a strange moment.

The kind of question that shouldn't belong in the middle of silence.
And yet — it fit perfectly.

The bow didn't twitch.

The arm didn't lower.
But Arjuna spoke.

Calmly. As if from beneath a warm river.

"No, Guru Dev."

A pause.

"I don't feel anything right now."

Drona's brow lifted. Slightly.
He leaned in — not invading, but listening *with his whole presence.*

"How long can you hold this state?"

Arjuna didn't rush the answer.

He didn't frown.
He didn't guess.
He simply… felt.

Time passed.

Then:

"I don't know, Guru Dev…"

Another pause. He breathed slowly.

"…but it feels warm."

His voice was distant, dreamy — but clean.

Like someone walking through the edge of a temple dream.

"Like I'm asleep. But awake."

He swallowed once, slowly.

"I don't feel the need for food or water."

A final breath.

"I feel… peaceful."

The words hung in the air like incense.
Soft. Lingering. Penetrating.

Behind Drona, the students said nothing.
But their eyes were wide.

Some were trembling.
Some pressing their palms together unconsciously.
As if what they were witnessing wasn't training —
But tapasya.

The kind seen in old stories.
The kind that made gods *pause.*

Drona nodded slowly.

His arms were crossed now.
But his heart… it wasn't still.

He was no longer looking at a student.
He was looking at something he hadn't seen in years.

Something ancient.
Something rare.

He stepped to the side, just slightly — out of the path of the bow's line.

His voice dropped, not in volume — but in age.
It sounded older now. Like it came from a deeper place in him.

"I once told you…" he said,
"The arrow will go where your eyes go."

He paused.

"Do you believe it now?"

There was no hesitation in the reply.

"I do."

Drona watched Arjuna's face — still smooth, still untouched by time.
But the voice…
The voice was no longer a boy's.

It carried conviction without force. A strange kind of still fire. Drona's head tilted slightly.

"Then why haven't you shot?" The question hovered. For a moment, it almost felt like a trap.

But Arjuna's voice came back,
quiet, sure — not defiant, not proud — just *true.*

"Because you asked me only to aim…"
"…not to shoot."

Silence.

Not empty — but full.
Heavy. Rooted.

A silence that spoke louder than applause, sharper than steel.

Drona closed his eyes.
A slow exhale left his lips.
And when they opened again — there was a smile.

Not wide.
Not showy.
But real.

A smile of recognition.

The kind only a master can give —
when he knows the one he's trained… has already stepped beyond him.

Drona stood in stillness for a long moment.
Then, without turning his head, he whispered to his assistant:

"Urnanabha."

The assistant stepped forward silently.
A small dagger was passed — its blade glinting briefly in the soft amber light.

Drona took it.
No expression. No sound.

He stepped toward Arjuna, who still stood —
locked in his stance,
bow drawn,
eyes unshaken.

Drona came so close, he could hear Arjuna's breath — slow, steady, like someone not aiming… but *being* the aim.

"Arjuna…" Drona said softly.

"Umm…" Arjuna replied, not blinking, not flinching.

"Are your shoulders paining?"
"No, Guruji."

"Do you feel any pain in your fingers?"
"No, Guruji."

Drona didn't respond.

Instead, he knelt — gently, almost reverently — and with the tip of the dagger, made a tiny cut near Arjuna's foot.

A single drop of blood welled up.
Crimson against dust.

"Do you feel that?" Drona asked.

"Feel what, Guru Dev?"
"Pain. In your foot."

"No, Guru Dev."

"What do you see?"

"The eye of the bird."

Drona stood tall.

His chest rose.
His face changed.
There was no smile — only pride so deep it couldn't find the surface.

He turned to the others — the 105 now standing like pillars behind him — and his voice rang out across the courtyard.

"Arjuna."

"Yes, Guru Dev?"

"Do you want to see if you can hit the target?"

A pause.

Then a calm, sacred whisper: "I'm waiting for that, Guru Dev." Drona's eyes narrowed.

"What did I say about seeing?" Arjuna didn't answer immediately.

But the response came — not from him alone. All 105 boys whispered in unison:

"नेत्रं मूलं विजयानाम्।"

(*Netraṁ mūlaṁ vijayānām.*) "The eye is the root of victory."

Drona nodded. Then softly, as if announcing fate:

"Arjuna."

"Gurudev."

"Can you take aim at the eye of the bird?"

Arjuna inhaled. A deep, long, focused breath. Not as if preparing to shoot — But as if beginning something. Something new. Something final. "Yes, Guru Dev. I see the eye."

Drona's voice dropped again. "What else do you see?"

"The eye, Guru Dev." Nothing else. Only that.

Drona's chin rose. His eyes sharpened. His spine straightened like a drawn bowstring.

And then —
he said the word that only masters say when they know destiny is listening. "**Aaghat.**"

"Strike."

One breath.

ZIP.

The sound cracked through the air like thunder. The arrow tore the silence open. Sharp. Clean. Unshaken.

It cut through the wind —A line of will drawn through time — And pierced the bird's eye.

Dead. Center.

For a moment, the world froze.

Even the wind paused. Even the trees leaned. Even the sky seemed to *watch*.

Then— "**HAR HAR**—!" Drona roared.

"—**MAHADEV**!!" the boys screamed in unison. A cry built in their chests.

First in Bhima, then Yuyutsu, then Vikarna, then all of them — Kaurava and Pandava alike.

And they erupted.

"HAR HAR—!" "—MAHADEV!!"

It wasn't just a chant.
It was an explosion.

The jungle came alive. Birds lifted like smoke.
Leaves rained down from trees.Monkeys howled and swung from branch to branch.
Even the earth itself seemed to drum beneath their feet.

Arjuna lowered his bow. His arms, steady. His breath, deep. His eyes… finally blinking, like waking from another world.

He turned. Walked slowly to Drona, And without a word — bowed low and touched his feet.

Drona looked down at him.

He didn't speak. He didn't need to. He just nodded…

…and then, in a voice only Arjuna could hear —
a whisper folded in reverence and recognition — he spoke:

"*Sham no Rudrah.*"
May Rudra be gentle with you. A blessing.A prayer. A seal.

And that's when the boys surged forward.

They didn't ask. They didn't plan. They lifted Arjuna onto their shoulders — like a king returning from war.

"*ARJUNA! ARJUNA! ARJUNA!*" they chanted.

Not with jealousy. Not with fear. But with fury and joy and brotherhood.

The jungle was roaring.Every corner. Every shadow. Every tree was ringing with it:

"HAR HAR MAHADEV!"

And at the heart of it — A boy who had not just struck a bird's eye. But had struck the nerve of destiny. And now — it was awake.

This is the story they still tell.

In gurukuls. In homes. Around fires beneath open skies.
In whispers and in thunder.

"What do you see?" Drona's question.

"The eye of the bird." Arjuna's answer.

CHAPTER 4

TO STRIKE WHAT WON'T STAY STILL

We ended with a question — **"What do you see?"**
And an answer sharp as silence —**"The eye of the bird."**

That was a story of stillness — of seeing without distraction.
But what if the target never stood still?
What if clarity had to pass through distortion?
What if you couldn't look at the eye at all — but only its shadow… in water?

This time, the target wasn't in the sky. It wasn't still.
It spun — a metal fish, high above, circling on a wheel that never stopped moving.
Round and round it went, like fate itself — refusing to rest.

But the archer wasn't allowed to look up.
He had to aim by looking down — into a pool of water.
There, in the shifting surface, he could see only a shadow. A flicker. A blur.
A lie that looked like the truth.

The Story of Draupadi's Swayamvara

In ancient Indian tradition, a **Swayamvara** was a sacred ceremony where a woman of royal or noble birth chose her husband — not through arrangement, but through **choice**.

The word *Swayam* means "self" and *Vara* means "groom" — so *Swayamvara* literally means *choosing one's own husband.*

Many kings would gather, hoping to win the bride through a challenge —
sometimes through strength, sometimes through skill, and sometimes, simply through her heart.

But this wasn't just about love or status. It was about **ability**. Only the one who could prove his worth — through wisdom, courage, or unmatched skill — would be chosen.

In a Swayamvara, it wasn't birth that mattered most. It was the fire within.

Long ago, there was a wise and powerful king named **Drupada** .

He had a daughter named **Draupadi**, known across kingdoms for her beauty, grace, and inner strength.

But before he was the father of a queen…
Drupada was a king built of fire and pride.

In his youth, he was a student.
And in that firelit gurukul, he had once sat shoulder to shoulder with **Drona** —
eating from the same leaf, reciting the same mantras, dreaming with the same hunger.

One night, under the silence of stars, he had declared with a boy's loyalty:
"When I become king, half my kingdom will be yours."

Words tossed into the wind. But the wind remembers.

Years passed. Power came.And with it — forgetfulness.

When Drona returned one day — poor, dust-covered, and hollow-eyed —
he didn't ask for land. He didn't speak of kingdoms or past promises.

He asked for **a single cow —a danam**, a humble gift, so he could feed his hungry son.

And that wasn't just a plea from a friend. It was a **king's duty** — to offer danam to Brahmins and scholars, those who preserved knowledge and passed it on.

But Drupada… had changed.

He no longer saw the sacred in such simplicity.

He saw a beggar where a friend once stood. And in a hall full of courtiers and warriors,
he rejected not just the request —but the very idea that this man was his equal.

"Friendship exists only between equals," Drupada said, cold and crowned.

Drona didn't argue. He didn't plead. He bowed, turned, and walked away. But fire had been lit inside him — slow and silent.

A Warning in the Stars

Some years later, an unusual message arrived .Not from spies. Not from enemies. But from within the palace itself. The royal priest, keeper of celestial rhythms, whispered:

"Your stars tremble. There is a turning.
A karmic shadow approaches — quiet but absolute.
You must perform the Ranachandi Homam — or risk everything."

A fierce ritual. Meant to awaken the goddess of war. To protect kings on the edge of fate.

But Drupada, steeped in wine and self-assurance, simply laughed.

"These priests... when fate is bored, they invent storms."

He dismissed the warning. Dismissed the ritual. Dismissed the silence.

Three Days Later – The First Crack

Just as the soft gold of *prātaḥkāla* (early morning) spilled across the eastern sky, a dust-covered rider arrived at the gates of *Kampilya* — the capital of *Pāñcāla* and seat of King Drupada.

The palace shadows were still long, the day not yet fully awake. The court had just gathered. Priests were finishing the morning *agnihotra*. The bells of the royal temple had not yet fallen silent.

The rider, smeared in ash and sweat, stumbled into the royal court — breathless, sunburnt, and pale.
He collapsed to one knee and spoke between gulps of air:

"Maharaj... A **platoon** — eighty, maybe a hundred men.

Armed. Chariots and cavalry. They crossed into *Vyāghrapura* before dawn — around the *brahma muhūrta*, perhaps 4 o'clock.
They are swift. If not already… they'll be on the outskirts of the capital within the next hour."

Drupada, calm as stone, asked, "Just a single platoon? No *maṇḍala sainya*? No siege caravans? "No larger force?"

"No, Maharaj. No siege machines, no supply lines. Just… a band.
Loud. No stealth. Like… noise pretending to be war."

Drupada's eyes narrowed, but his breath did not change. He turned to his *mantrī*, the venerable *Somadeva*, a man whose wisdom was as unhurried as a mountain river.

Somadeva pressed his palms together and said:

"What arrives without stealth may still carry shadow.
It sounds immature… but so have many traps that tore down kings

Chhālaḥ api sāmarthyam bibharti — Even a deception can carry strength."**

He paused, then added gravely:

"Let us remember what *Rāvaṇa* taught his son *Meghnāda*: 'अवमानः शत्रोः प्रमादस्य मूलम्।'

(Avamānaḥ śatroḥ pramādasya mūlam)
'To underestimate the enemy is the seed of disaster.'"

The morning sun had barely lit the spires of Kampilya, but a shadow had already entered its gates — not of soldiers, but of misjudgment.

"Mahārāja," Somadeva concluded, **"this may not be war. But it could very well be its beginning."**

Inside the Royal Court – A Growing Unease

As the dust of the rider's warning settled into silence, unease swirled like smoke in the court.

Minister Jayantha, elder and seasoned, broke first:
"We were watching the wrong borders. I accept it — this is a failure in surveillance."

Minister Agnimitra clenched his fists.
"No… not just surveillance. *Judgement.* We grew too confident. Too proud. We assumed no one would dare."

A third minister, *Vakul*, younger but sharp, stood abruptly — his eyes wet with shame.

"Mahārāja… I have no excuse."
He removed his *angavastra* and placed it on the stone floor.

"I was tasked to report troop movements from the western ridge. I dismissed three border sightings as wandering hunters.
That was three days ago."

He stepped forward.

"I failed. I request that my head be offered to the throne. Let the people know we still hold truth above comfort."

The court fell into stunned silence.

Even Somadeva looked away — not in disapproval, but in respect.

Drupada raised a hand.
His voice was quiet. Not soft — quiet like a sword just before the draw.

"We are not butchers of conscience, Vakul. But your honesty is armour to this kingdom. Let it be known."

He turned slowly to face the hall.

"But here is the truth we must not ignore."
He looked at Somadeva.
"What do we *know*?"

Somadeva exhaled — steady, composed.

"Nothing. No name. No symbol. No purpose.

We have no *śatru-bhoj*. We are blind. And when kings move blind — empires fall."

Drupada's gaze turned to steel.

"Then let us not walk — let us strike.
If we are to respond in darkness, we shall respond with fire."

The King's Decision

Drupada rose from his throne.

For a flicker of a moment, regret crossed his face —The memory of **the old Brahmin**, humiliated before the court. The ritual he had refused. The silence that followed.

But pride returned to its seat. "This is no time for regret. Let the enemy know that Panchala does not blink."

He turned to his **army chief**, **Commander Veeryananda**, and spoke clearly:

"I order the deployment of the **Vajra Vyuha**. Full war formation. This is not a skirmish — this is a message."

Veeryananda blinked.

"Maharaj… A **Vajra Vyuha**? For just one platoon?"

Drupada's voice cut like steel.

"Yes. Because this is not for them.
It is for our people — to show them that their king does not blink.
And for the gods — to show them that *Dharma* still has defenders."

Veeryananda bowed. "As you command, Maharaj."

The Vajra Vyuha Awakens

Veeryananda walked to the ramparts and raised his hand.

" Raise the **Agni-dhvaja**!" From every tower of Kampilya, **yellow war flags with blazing fire symbols** unfurled in the wind. Trumpets blared. Drums rolled like thunder.

" Activate Vajra Vyuha!" he roared.

A voice echoed it from the walls. Then another. Then a hundred.

Soldiers moved as one — forming the **diamond-shaped battle formation**, an unbreakable mix of offense and defense.

Drupada rode to the center of the formation, under his **golden flag** marked by the **Hamsa** — the royal swan.

In minutes, the formation locked into place like a puzzle of war. Chariots flanked the outer arc. Cavalry took the edges. Infantry filled the gaps.

The First Clash

The enemy came charging. But they were broken before the outer layer was breached. And they turned back to escape.

"Who were these fools?" Drupada asked, unimpressed.

A scout replied, "Our men heard names whispered... **Suyodhana**, **Karna**... perhaps young warriors from **Hastinapura**."

Drupada scoffed. "Children."

Veeryananda returned.

"They've fled, Maharaj. Crossed back over the border."

Somadeva added, "Shall we stand down?"

Drupada hesitated. His instincts stirred.

"Not yet. Let the silence breathe first.
Sometimes... the second strike wears no footsteps."

Veeryananda agreed, wordlessly.

And then it came.

A high, hissing sound — **like fate tearing through fabric**.

An **arrow** pierced the air and struck **just one inch** above Drupada's crown — slamming into the **flagpole**.

The pole cracked. The golden flag — the **swan of Panchala** — bent but didn't fall.

The court stood frozen.

A scroll was tied to the shaft.

A guard pulled it, unrolled it — and read aloud:

"Surrender your kingdom.
Accept Yudhishthira as rightful king.
Or face what comes."

No emblem. No seal. Just one name — handwritten in the curve of a boy's pride.

Arjuna
Brother of Yudhishthira.

A second arrow came — sharp, hissing, and absolute. It didn't aim for flesh. It aimed for pride.

It struck the **eye of the Hamsa** on Drupada's flag. The banner shook. A murmur rippled through the formation.

This time, a scroll was tied with it.

"If you accept the offer, raise a white flag.
Step down from your chariot, and walk to the left corner of your Vajra Vyuha and stand at the Peepal tree.
Do this before Rāhukāla begins — you have approximately twenty minutes.
If not… be ready to face the worst."
— Signed, Arjuna

Drupada's face stiffened.
He snatched the spyglass, scanning the horizon.

His generals, captains, and advisors followed suit, raising their scopes, looking straight ahead — from where the arrow's angle suggested it had come.

Nothing.

Just trees. Air. Silence.

But the message was clear.

A choice.
A countdown.
And a threat spoken in perfect stillness.

Somadeva murmured, **"They've given us a window, Mahārāja.**
A false mercy… or a final test."

The silence stretched.
Drupada didn't speak. He didn't move.
Only the sound of distant birds, and the dry hum of a kingdom thinking.

The wind shifted slightly — and even that felt watched.

And then — *Rāhukāla* began.

No white flag rose.

What followed was not war.

It was execution.

Seven arrows — launched together, to seven hidden directions —

cut the air like synchronized whispers of death.

They struck not with rage, but with *intent.*

Each arrow tore through the chestplates of seven mounted captains,
the metal splitting like paper.

But they didn't stop there.

They continued — piercing into the warhorses beneath,
sinking **half an inch deep** into the narrow cleft where **loin meets croup** —
that precise, sacred notch of motion.

The shots were impossibly perfect.

Each arrow transfixed two beings — man and beast —
pinning them together in a grotesque stillness.

The captains did not fall.

They remained upright in their saddles —
anchored by the arrow shafts that speared through their torsos into their mounts.

But their heads —
their heads hung back, limp, swaying like offerings in the wind.

The horses screamed and bolted.

They raced across the formation in terror,
dragging their riders — still seated, still armored — like cursed statues atop their backs.

From above, it looked like the *Vajra Vyuha* had grown seven black wings and lost its soul.

The formation cracked.

Not from a charge.
Not from fire.
But from the silent severing of command.

Seven minds.
Seven spines of strategy.
Gone.

And with them, the balance of the thunderbolt.

Drupada turned the scope quickly — nothing again.
Just haze. Hills. Stillness.

He glanced at Commander Veeryananda.

A silent nod.

But no command followed.
And the archers… hesitated.

They stood ready — bows drawn, breath held —

but no one fired.

Their target was too far.
And they had already seen what the enemy archer could do.

"Movement!" someone called out.

Scopes shifted.

"Not an army… Less than ten. One giant in front. Two chariots. Riders on the flanks."

Drupada focused in.
The front-runner — massive, bare-bodied, hair wild.

"Who is this beast?"

No one answered.

One archer whispered,
"That's where the arrows came from…"

Another lowered his bow.

**"We can't even reach that distance.
Not with that kind of precision."**

The backline shifted — not in formation, but in fear.
Some archers looked to their captains.
But the captains were gone — dead, still mounted, held upright by the arrows that killed them.

"Should we move forward?" someone asked.

"Close the gap?"

"Who approves that?" came the reply.

Silence.

A few archers stepped forward instinctively, then stopped — caught between duty and dread.

And from the distant hills, the small enemy force kept advancing —
calm, coordinated, and completely in control.

Drupada lowered the spyglass, then raised it again, this time focusing on the approaching chariots.

Beside him, Somadeva narrowed his eyes and said quietly,
"Chestnut horses… The rider's thin… focused. The man beside him—
he's seated. Steady. Looks like… Yudhishthira."

Drupada frowned.
"He brought no army?"

Somadeva continued, voice sharpening,
"Just five spears.
That chariot carries only five spears… and yet he rides straight toward a full battalion."

Drupada turned the scope to the next chariot — drawn by white horses.

His brow tightened.
A whisper escaped his lips:

**"So… he is Arjuna.
And that is the bow."**

Before Drupada could finish scanning the rest of the formation—

FWUUUMP!

A spear flew through the air — fast and sharp, like it knew exactly where to go.

It slipped between the two front horses of Drupada's chariot, without touching them. In the very next second, it smashed into the right wheel with a loud CRACK!

The wooden wheel broke into pieces. Spokes flew off. The axle twisted. The chariot suddenly tilted to the right, dragging unevenly over the rocky ground.

The horses reared up, panicked. Their hooves kicked the air. But the charioteer, strong and experienced, held the reins tight. He tried his best to stop them.

For a moment, he managed to hold them.

But then — the second spear came.

Even faster.

This one didn't go for the chariot — it went for the man driving it.

It hit the charioteer right in the chest. The spear went deep, and the force of it threw him backward, off his seat.

He didn't scream. Just gasped, as if all the air had left his body.

He fell back, dying — but his legs were still moving, shaking from the shock.

And one of his feet kicked the lead horse.

That was it.

The already frightened horses lost control.

They shrieked — wild, high-pitched cries — and began to run like fire, dragging the broken chariot with them.

The chariot was now on only one wheel, tilted badly to the side, scraping the ground.

Dust flew. Sparks flew. Blood dripped from the dying charioteer.

Then came a strange sound.

Not metal. Not wind. A whistle.

Soft at first, then rising, like someone calling the horses from far away — not with force, but with power.

The horses heard it.
And they ran even faster.

As if something was chasing them that no one could see.

The **horses ran wild**, dragging the broken chariot faster and faster.

They didn't stop for anyone.

They didn't follow orders.

They **rushed straight through the heart of the Vajra Vyuha** — the tightly guarded diamond formation that Drupada himself had ordered.

Soldiers jumped aside.

Chariots moved out of the way.

No one dared stop the king's horses —
because even they didn't know who or what was really controlling them now.

The chariot bounced and leaned heavily to one side. **Drupada held on tight**, gripping the edge with both hands. His armor clanged. Dust and blood filled the air.

Then — it happened.

Another strange **whistling sound** rose in the air.

This one was **louder**, like the call of a storm.

A third **spear** flew in front of the horses and landed **just one foot ahead** — deep into the ground.

And the horses **froze**.

Like they had hit an invisible wall. Just infront of peepal tree.

Their eyes were wide. Their bodies stiff. They stopped so suddenly that the chariot rocked forward and almost tipped over.

Drupada's army began to move — trying to protect their king — but it was too late.

The **giant man** — the one they had seen earlier — now stepped into the field.

He was bare-chested. His muscles were huge. His eyes were wild.

With a roar, he **pulled out a banyan tree from the ground** and **threw it** at the soldiers coming to protect Drupada.

Thud!
Men flew. Shields shattered.

Then he began to **throw more trees**, like they were nothing.

Soldiers screamed and scattered. The formation was breaking.

And now…

From between the clouds of dust, **Arjuna** appeared.

He had laid his bow aside.

He was **walking calmly**, with **bare hands**, through the chaos.

Not rushing.

Not looking around.

Just walking — like a lion who knows no one can stop him.

Everyone on the battlefield stopped.

Even Drupada felt his feet wanting to move **backwards**.

But it was too late.

Arjuna walked straight to the broken chariot.
He looked up at Drupada, then calmly reached out and **grabbed the king by the belt**.

He **pulled him slightly** forward, then — with both hands — **tore open his chest armor**, ripping the straps with ease.

Next, he reached for Drupada's **pearl necklace**, grabbed it, and **pulled hard**.

The necklace broke.
The pearls fell to the ground.
The **crown rolled away**, landing at the hooves of the horses.

And **Drupada fell**.

Like a bag of rice, loose and helpless.

Before he could rise, Arjuna **grabbed his hair** and **dragged him** through the dirt.

His knees scraped. His elbows bled. His royal robe tore at the sides.

As **Arjuna dragged Drupada** toward his chariot, the battlefield still held its breath — stunned by what it had just seen.

But before he reached, the **two horsemen — Nakula and Sahadeva — whistled again.**

Not once. Twice.

And this time… it wasn't just a sound.
It was a command.

The animals in the Panchala army — the horses, the elephants, even the hounds — all began to stir.

The entire Vajra Vyuha broke apart.

Warhorses twisted their necks. Elephants trumpeted and turned. Chariots tangled. Men shouted. Nothing responded.

The entire formation that once looked unbreakable now looked like it had been **cursed**.

No fight. No order. Just chaos.

And in the middle of it, Arjuna walked straight.

At last, Arjuna reached the chariot where the **giant warrior** — now clearly **Bhima** — stood waiting with a smile full of teeth.

"Welcome, O King," Bhima said, as if greeting an honored guest.
"I hope the ride wasn't too rough."

Arjuna **threw Drupada** into the chariot like a sack of grain, climbed up beside him, and without a word, placed his **left foot on the king's neck**.

Drupada lay there — silent, dusty, broken.

Bhima leaned in and said with a mocking grin,
"That's **Yudhishthira** in the other chariot — your new master.
And the foot pressing your pride? That's **Arjuna**, the one you once called a boy.
And the ones who is making your army dance now? **Nakula and Sahadeva.**"

Without wasting another breath, Arjuna looked Commanded.

"**Pratyāgacchhata!**" *Fall back.*

Nakula, Sahadeva, Bhima, and Yudhishthira turned their chariots — but not Arjuna.

He simply **looked at Bhima**. Just a glance.

And Bhima smiled — not with mischief, but with pride.

Arjuna didn't follow.

He **turned his chariot**, with **Drupada underfoot**, and rode straight through what remained of the once-proud army of Panchala.

He didn't need to dodge them.

They **moved on their own**.

Some out of fear. Some out of shame. Some out of disbelief.

He reached the **gates of Kampilya**, stopped, and looked up at the palace.

"Hmmm..." he said, softly.
That was it.

Then he circled the palace — slowly — like a predator marking its ground.

His **white horses trotted** in perfect rhythm. His chariot made no noise. His gaze never broke.

People watched from windows, roofs, balconies.
Their king — underfoot.

The conqueror — silent, calm, untouchable.

He then rode into the heart of the city.

And at a **small junction**, the chariot came to a stop — without any signal.

People stared in shock. Some children hid behind doors. Some elders whispered.

"Is he using a **Sammohan Astra**?" one old sage muttered. "How else could a king become a doormat without a fight?"

Arjuna stepped down — still calm.

He didn't raise his hand.

He simply looked at a boy nearby, and the boy ran off to fetch water for the horses.

Arjuna watched.

Not his enemies. Not the crowd.

He watched his **horses** — as they drank.

An old woman appeared, holding a small leaf bowl with sesame seeds and jaggery.

Her hands were shaking.

Arjuna turned to her, bowed with joined palms, and accepted the offering.

He chewed slowly — calmly — as if nothing around him mattered.

A Warrior's Ritual

Once the horses were done, Arjuna walked up to them.

With care, he **rubbed one horse's front leg**, from elbow to hoof.
Then the second leg, same way.

Two strokes. Gentle. Firm.

He moved to the second horse.
Did the same.

Then he took their ears in his hands — **brushed them softly** — like a warrior preparing them for the next journey.

From what was left of the jaggery in his leaf bowl, he **fed each horse** a small bite.

Then he washed his face, his hands — letting the water fall softly to the dust below.

He took out **three gold coins** and gave them to the **old lady**, bowing to her once more.

Then he gave **five silver coins** to the **young boy** who had watered the horses.

No words.

Just silence. And gratitude.

Departure

Then he climbed back onto the chariot.

Placed his foot once again on Drupada's neck.

And with the sun behind him, the horses galloped forward — out of **Panchala's gates**.

The people watched until the dust swallowed him.

Arjuna never looked back.

The boy had come.
The king had fallen.
And the city had witnessed a silence more powerful than war.

They rode not to the heart of Hastinapura, but to a **small palace**, built far from noise — where discipline stood guard and pride had no voice.

It was **simple**. **Royal.**

And waiting.

At the gate stood **his brothers**.

Lined like mountains.
Still as stone.
Arms crossed. Eyes watching.

Nakula. Sahadeva. Bhima. Yudhishthira.

Not one of them spoke.

The **white chariot** rolled in, and the horses came to a gentle halt.

Arjuna stood still for a moment, looking at the courtyard.

Then, with slow precision, he **opened the chariot door**.

He placed his foot on the back of Drupada's neck…
And with one swift motion — **slid it forward to the throat**, and gave a short flick.

Thud.

The king of Panchala **spilled out** onto the stone.

He groaned.
Tried to rise.
But **Arjuna was already out**, already walking — already **lifting him by the hair**. He dragged him across the open courtyard.

The stones were hot.
The wind was dry.
Drupada's **robes were torn**, his skin scraped raw, his breaths short and bitter.

Every few steps, he tried to resist — but Arjuna didn't even look down.

The **Pandava warrior's grip** was like iron.
And the walk — like a ritual.

By the time Drupada was brought to the **center of the courtyard**, there was:

- No crown.
- No silk.
- No guards.
- No memory of a throne.

Only a name. And the **weight of shame.**

"**Guru Dev!**" Nakula called. His voice was clear. Young. Devoted. And from the corridor's shade… A figure emerged. Drona Appears Tall. Thin. Straight as a blade left unsheathed for years.

He walked slowly.
His hands folded behind his back.
His steps silent, but each one landed like a bell.

Drona. The teacher. The outcast. The insulted. He wore simple robes, but his eyes — his eyes were **older than fire**.

He did not rush. He did not smile.

He stopped at the edge of the courtyard and looked at the man on the ground.

The man who had once been humiliated in this very kingdom.

He walked forward — not with revenge, but with stillness. Like a river returning to the sea.

The brothers bowed. Drona's wife stepped out, carrying a small vessel of water. She offered it to Arjuna. Arjuna bowed low. Took it in both hands and drank.

Drona looked at the kneeling man.

"What is this creature?" he asked, voice soft, dangerous.

Bhima stepped forward, grinning.

"This? Just a moment ago, he was king."

"And now?"

"Now?" Bhima shrugged. "A slave, if generous. A beggar, if honest."

Drona chuckled. A small sound. The kind that carries more weight than a scream.

"Sahadeva," he said, "what is his name?" Sahadeva smiled — but said nothing.

Drona stepped forward.

"Slave," he said, looking down."What is your name?"

Drupada stayed silent.

Eyes cast low.

Breathing shallow.

Drona looked to his son.

"Ashwatthama?"

The young man came forward. "Yes, Pitaśri?"

"Recognize him?"

Ashwatthama squinted. "Vaguely. Feels like someone from an old story."

He turned — theatrical — and returned with a cup of milk. Not cow's milk. Donkey's milk.

He forced it to Drupada's lips.

"Drink, Maharaj," he whispered. "It's the least we could offer our royal guest."

Drupada coughed. Swallowed. A tear escaped. No one mocked him. Because no one needed to. Drona crouched beside him. Whispered. "Now… say it. What is your name?"

"…Drupada."

"*Drupada Maharaj… Panchala Naresh…*"
He tasted the titles like old wine gone sour.

"Hmm. Quite a personality. Quite a name. Quite an arrogance…"

He leaned closer, almost whispering now. "…and quite a price."

He stood again — slowly, like a mountain rising from meditation.

"Tell me," he said, arms folded, voice echoing through the marble,
"How does a man who once spoke of kingdoms and oaths and childhood vows…
end up kneeling in the dirt, drinking donkey's milk?"

Drona whispered once. Then again. A quiet reminder of what equality truly costs.

Drupada didn't respond.
Because his voice — like his pride — had cracked. He looked up. And in that single glance —
the tears, the dust, the torn silk, the silence — he said nothing.

Drona looked at him. Long. Deep. Silent. And then — as suddenly as a sword returned to its sheath — he nodded.

"It is enough."

He raised his hand. Servants moved. Water was brought. Clean clothes. A warm meal.
Drupada was lifted. Not by force this time — but with care.

Because even pride, once broken, deserves rest. Drona himself laid a mat.
Asked for rice to be served.
Sat beside him, eating not as enemies — but as old friends who had finally spoken.

When the meal was done, Drona stood again. His eyes met Arjuna's.

"Take him home."

Bhima stepped forward first — silent, respectful. Nakul brought the chariot.

Arjuna helped Drupada to his feet — not as a conqueror now, but as a man who had done what needed to be done. No words were exchanged. Because some endings don't require them.

They led the king back to his city. To his gates. To what remained. But one truth lingered — unspoken, unforgettable: That day… Panchala didn't lose a king. It witnessed a *disciple's promise kept.* And a *guru's wound forgiven*

That night, after the chariot returned him to his palace —

after the silence in the halls had grown too heavy to bear — Drupada sat alone.

Not on a throne. On the floor. On cold stone, with no crown, no ornaments, no distractions.
Only thoughts. Only that name. **Arjuna.**

His mind kept circling back —
not to the humiliation,
but to the *manner* of it.
The focus. The detachment.
The terrifying beauty of a warrior who moved like truth itself.

"I don't want vengeance anymore,"
Drupada whispered into the dark.
"I want meaning. I want connection."

"I want Arjuna… as my own blood." And so, he rose.

He began to search — not for warriors or spies — but for **brahmins.** He summoned every priest, every scholar, every sage who had once whispered mantras to fire and made gods listen. He travelled in secret, dressed as a seeker. He knocked on forest ashrams. He questioned pilgrims.
He sent emissaries to distant hermitages.

Days passed. Then weeks. Until at last — he found them.
Yaja and Upayaja.

Two brothers. Silent. Soft-spoken. Masters of the sacred fire. Keepers of ancient yagna-vidya.
They did not crave wealth. They did not serve kings. But when Drupada knelt before them — not as a ruler, but as a man torn open by longing —
they listened.

Yaja asked only one question: "Is this yagna for power… or for dharma?" Drupada folded his hands. His voice trembled. "It is for a son to restore balance. And a daughter…to bind me to the one man who burned away my pride and showed me who I truly am."

The brothers looked at each other. Then nodded.

So the site was chosen. A yagna-shala built from sacred wood and silence.
No gold. No banners. Only fire.

And when the flames rose — so did a destiny that would shape the future of kingdoms.

Because from that fire… would come **Dhrishtadyumna** — the slayer of Drona.
And **Draupadi** — the woman born of flame, the woman who would one day walk into Arjuna's life not as a wish — but as a vow fulfilled.

When the time came for Draupadi to marry, Drupada prepared the grandest swayamvara the world had seen. But fate, it seemed, had a cruel script to play.

News came that Arjuna — and his brothers — had perished in a fire. A house of wax. A trap.
Ashes, they said. No survivors. The dream — of alliance, of atonement, of Arjuna as his son-in-law —burned away in that same fire.

But not **hope.**

Drupada's heart still held one ember. So, he crafted a test — not of strength alone, but of something rarer. Something divine.

A test of **vision.** Of **stillness.** Of **perception beyond the obvious.**

In the center of the royal court, before kings and warriors from every corner of Aryavarta,
stood a colossal bow — carved from dark sandalwood, heavy as dharma itself.
Above it, suspended on a tall pole, spun a golden fish — glinting in the morning light.
Below, a bowl of rippling water.
The only way to strike the target… was by seeing its *reflection*.

To win Draupadi's hand, a suitor had to pierce the eye of the fish —without looking at it directly. A task so impossible…

only a man who had once hit the eye of a wooden bird while the world disappeared could even understand what it meant.

Warriors came. Chests broad, voices louder than their aim. Some couldn't even string the bow.
Others lifted it, but missed — not just the fish, but themselves.

Some trembled before they even touched the string. Because **true stillness** doesn't come from silence —it comes from the absence of *self.* And then… a quiet Brahmin stepped forward.

No gold. No silk. Just dust on his feet and purpose in his stride. He moved like a question the world had forgotten how to ask. Calm. Unshaken. Not afraid. Because fear lives only in those who are unsure why they've come.

He didn't boast. He didn't pause.

It was **Arjuna.**

Alive. But hidden — wrapped in humility like armor.

He circled the bow once — like a friend returning home. He closed his eyes.
Whispered a prayer — not to win, but to *see clearly.*

Then — with breath like wind over still water — he lifted the bow. Not with force.

With *alignment.*

He didn't look up. Didn't search the sky. His eyes stayed rooted in the bowl of water.
The reflection rippled, swayed — but he remained steady.

Because Arjuna didn't need to see the target. He needed only to see *himself* not in the way.

Twang.

The arrow flew. Straight. Sharp. Unwavering. It pierced the fish's eye. Perfect. Final. Without hesitation. The golden fish spun once —then fell.

The court gasped. And then… silence. The kind of silence that happens when fate exhales.

Draupadi stood. Eyes wide. Heart still. She walked toward the Brahmin with a garland in her hands. She didn't know yet — but *something in her did.*And when she reached him, and placed the garland around his neck, the court shifted.

Because the world had just witnessed something ancient: A warrior not winning by strength,
but by **clarity.**

That day, Arjuna didn't just win a bride. He won *recognition.* He won a place in every warrior's story — not because he shouted, but because he **saw.**

CHAPTER 5

THE ONE WHO STANDS BETWEEN

What happens when two powerful men—once equals—become strangers?

One becomes a king. The other, a teacher. But the deeper story isn't about titles or thrones.
It's about how they *see* each other… and how they're seen by the one in between.

Drona and Drupada both looked at Arjuna and saw a weapon. But Arjuna was more than that.

He was a mirror. A reflection.

He did not react from emotion, but from **alignment**—of knowledge, intention, and timing.

He treated both men differently. Not because of their power, but because of their posture.

To Drona, who came with humility—Arjuna bowed. To Drupada, who stood on pride—Arjuna offered dust.

Because Arjuna doesn't respond to what you once were.
He reacts to what you are *now*.

In any civilization, peace is the dream. But peace is not passive. It must be protected, maintained, upheld. And that's where warriors come in.

The true warrior is not the one who desires war.
It's the one who holds it back... until there is no other choice.

Peace is only possible in two ways:
when there are no enemies, or when enemies are understood, managed, or defeated.

To do either, the warrior must not only fight. He must **see**.

That's why Arjuna's greatest lessons weren't about destruction.
They were about *perception*.

His first test was simple.

A bird. A branch. And a question from his teacher.

"What do you see?" Others answered with trees, clouds, feathers, leaves. But Arjuna said, "I see only the eye." That was enough.

Mastery does not come from seeing *more*. It comes from seeing *right*.

Later, at Draupadi's swayamvara, the test evolved. Now the target moved.

A golden fish spinning above. Its reflection flickering in a bowl of water.

This was no longer about strength. It was about stillness in chaos.

The fish wasn't chosen at random. It represented human emotion—restless, reactive, ever-moving. Fish never close their eyes. They feel everything and forget nothing.

The water? That was the heart—reflecting, rippling, trembling.

To aim through that was to declare: "My mind is calmer than the world around me." And deeper still— The eye wasn't just a point to hit. It was a **perspective**.

The enemy's world, his truth, his vision. To hit that eye was to place your truth inside his field of view. To make him see what he had refused to see. That's what enmity really is—*a failure to see each other.*

You don't always need to kill the enemy. Sometimes, you need to kill the *distance between perspectives.* This deeper understanding appears again and again in our history.

Take Subhas **Chandra Bose.**

He knew India wouldn't gain freedom by begging. But he also knew war wasn't just about armies—it was about optics. His Azad Hind Fauj wasn't built with just weapons. It was built with vision. A new identity planted inside the eyes of the oppressors: that India would rise, and the chains would break.

Look at **Maharana Pratap.**

He stood alone against a tidal empire, not because he had more men, but because he refused to be seen as less. He understood that surrender once—even in peace— would rewrite the future in defeat. His war was not for territory. It was to guard the **dignity of perspective.**

And **Chhatrapati Shivaji**?

A warrior king, yes, but also a master of perception. He struck not when provoked, but when precision called. He saw the gaps others missed; the fears others ignored. He didn't overpower. He out-saw.

Their victories weren't just victories of the sword. They were victories of **sight**.

Because the one who sees deepest… commands the war *before* it begins.

Even in the Mahabharata, Krishna held this truth.

He could've ended the battle with a single breath. But he chose to wait, guide, advise, offer peace again and again. He asked for five villages. Nothing more. But they could not see. So the bowstring had to speak.

When vision fails, war begins.

Arjuna stood in that space—
Between silence and strike.
Between humility and pride.
Between understanding and violence.

He was not born to destroy. He was shaped to act *only* when destruction became the last truth.

That is the mark of the real warrior.

To avoid war as long as possible. But when it comes— To enter it with vision, not vengeance.

The arrow is not the weapon.
The eye is.

Because before every war, before every fall, before every decision—

There is a moment.
A moment where someone could have seen clearly… and chose not to.

The world doesn't begin with fighting. It begins with *seeing*.

And so does truth.

And have you ever wondered…
why, in our ancient stories, the target is always the **eye**?

Not the heart. Not the throat. Not the head. But *the eye*.
The smallest mark. The most impossible shot. And yet—the only one that matters.

Because the eye is not just a point. It is a **portal**.
A shimmering slit between two worlds. To aim for the eye… is to do something far more dangerous than kill. It is to **be seen**.

The moment your arrow pierces that eye, you are no longer a stranger.
You are **inside**.
Inside their sight.
Inside their story.
Inside the very lens through which they shape their truth.

And once your truth enters their view—
there is no turning away.
They cannot unsee it.
They cannot un-know you.

And so, the enemy doesn't fall in blood. He falls in **revelation**.

War doesn't end with surrender. It ends in that quiet gasp—

when the one who opposed you realizes he is looking at **himself** through your aim.
And what he sees… is not a threat. But a reflection.

That's why the masters never taught us to aim at flesh.
They taught us to aim at **sight**.
Because when you can shoot into the eye—
cleanly, precisely, unshaking—
you don't just win. You **merge**.

And suddenly, there is no other side.
No battle.
No enemy.

Only understanding.

Because the arrow was never made to destroy. It was made to **deliver**— a piece of your world
into theirs. And that… is what the greatest warriors knew.
They weren't aiming at targets.
They were aiming at **awakening**.

And throughout history, a rare few truly *saw* —
not just with eyes, but with **vision**.
They looked beyond the battlefield.
Beyond the obvious.
Beyond their own lifetime. And because they saw more —
they built more. Not with steel. But with **clarity**.

Raja Raja Chola I (Reign: 985–1014 CE) – The Emperor Who Engineered Time

Far in the south, in the land of rivers and temples,
stood a king who did not rule with fear —but with *alignment*.

- Raja Raja Chola I didn't just command armies — he **orchestrated civilization**.
- He built the monumental **Brihadeeswara Temple** in Thanjavur (completed in **1010 CE**) — a structure so mathematically precise and spiritually aligned, it still stuns the modern world.
- He reorganized **village assemblies**, strengthened **irrigation**, funded **healthcare**, and expanded **maritime diplomacy** across Southeast Asia.
- His kingdom was not ruled from the top down — it flowed outward, like vision turned into policy.

We don't remember how many enemies he defeated.
We remember how **he saw far beyond them.**

Rawal Jaisal (Founded Jaisalmer in 1156 CE) – The Seer of the Sands

Centuries later, in the dry throat of the Thar Desert, another man stood — not on green fields, but on **barren gold**.

- **Rawal Jaisal**, in **1156 CE**, founded the fortress-city of **Jaisalmer** — not by accident, but by a kind of **vision only the desert teaches**.
- Where others saw heat, thirst, and isolation, he saw **safety**, **silence**, and **trade**.
- Jaisal built his citadel on a cliff, surrounded by sand, invisible to invaders but **irreplaceable to caravans**.
- With **no rivers to feed him, no forests to shield him**, he turned dust into defense and **silence into survival**.

We don't remember him for conquest.
We remember him for *where he chose to see what no one else did.*

The Legacy of Seeing

These men didn't lead because they were loud.
They led because they *saw*.

- One built a temple that still speaks to the skies.
- One raised a golden fortress that still gleams through sandstorms.

They remind us — you don't need to move armies to move history.
You need **vision**.

Just seeing — the first stage of truth —can lift civilizations, protect futures, and outlive empires.

Because the one who sees clearly, leads gently. And is remembered forever.

So if you're wondering where our journey begins...**It begins here.**

Not with conquest. Not with belief. Not even with questions.

It begins with a quiet gaze. With the stillness of a mind that chooses to look deeper.

Because the key is not command.The key is not certainty.

The key… is seeing.

CHAPTER 6

THE KEY IS SEEING

Metaphorically, because the *cornea* is fully developed and doesn't need to grow, it may lead us to assume that our perspective is already complete and requires no further updates. Similarly, a person might believe their viewpoint is final and comprehensive, feeling there is no need to consider other perspectives. This mindset results in our view being filled with blind spots.

Imagine you're buying your dream home today. You've finished all the paperwork, paid the previous owner or dealer, and settled taxes and fees with the government, officially putting the property under your name. Your family and friends have congratulated you on this achievement. This transaction seems to prove that you fully own the place.

However, could there be things we haven't thought about? Are you truly the sole owner of this place, or are there more complex aspects to consider?

Throughout this process, we have only viewed it from a human perspective. You've made deals with other humans who acknowledge your ownership. However, the same location might also be the territory of other creatures. In their own ways, these creatures might have acquired rights to ownership through their own processes.

Have you ever thought about who else might be living in your house besides you and your family? It turns out, your home could be an active territory for a variety of creatures, big and small.

In the house you live in, there are multiple territories. One place represents multiple worlds. I have provided a broader example by considering other creatures besides humans. If we focus solely on humans, imagine living in a place with lots of farms nearby. That makes your home part of the farming world. Or maybe you live in a fancy city area where everything seems shiny and expensive. That's a different world altogether. Some homes are in areas where powerful people, like politicians, live. It's a bit like being in their territory. And then there are places where people have strong beliefs or follow certain rules. That shapes the way they live and see the world.

I want to draw your attention to a point—that if you just start observing one thing deeply or widely, even something as ordinary as your house, it will slowly connect you to various territories, the world, and the universe. When you pick something up and take a closer look, you'll realize that the deeper you look, the wider your understanding becomes, and the wider you look, the deeper your understanding grows.

No matter where you start your journey, it will ultimately lead you through all aspects and bring you back to yourself.

This is the first stage of seeing something. And one story that illustrates this beautifully is the story of Krishna [kri-i-sh-nuh]and the mud.

The Mouth That Contained Everything

During his early childhood, Krishna was known for his mischief. Yasoda [Yaa-SHOW-Daa], Krishna's mother, adored him more than her own life. Every day, villagers would come with complaints, but Yasoda would dismiss them with a smile, charmed by her son's innocent face.

One day, Krishna was playing with his brother Balaram and their friends, the Gopala's. In the middle of their games, Krishna picked up a lump of mud and ate it. The Gopalas ran to Yasoda, alarmed, shouting, "Krishna is eating mud!"

Yasoda, anxious and angry, rushed to the scene. She grabbed Krishna by his tiny arms, scolding him. "Why did you eat mud, Krishna?"

Innocently, with his eyes trembling like a frightened bird, Krishna replied, "I didn't eat mud, Mother. They're lying. If you don't believe me, look into my mouth."

Yasoda, wanting to believe him but aware of his playful nature, said, "Open your mouth."

Krishna obeyed.

At first, she saw what any mother would expect: a small pink tongue, soft cheeks, a row of white baby teeth. But between the gaps of his teeth, something caught her eye—a smear of mud. But this mud felt different.

She squinted, leaning closer, focusing on that little brown smudge near his gums.

It looked like ordinary mud—but also like something more. She stared at it. It stared back.

Tiny specks of dust sparkled like stars. She saw what looked like mountain ranges stretching across the inner surface of Krishna's cheek. Rivers ran over his tongue. Clouds swirled between his teeth.

She began questioning:

"Is this the same mud Gopalas said he ate?"
"Is this the same mud I walk on every day?"
"Is this the mud that smells of the first rain?"
"Is this the same dust that feeds trees, animals, and humans alike?"
"Is this mud under oceans too? Does it become mountains and deserts?"

The more she looked, the more it revealed.

She saw the earth's layers moving, tectonic plates shifting, volcanoes erupting. Mountains like arrows pierced the sky and flew across space. Oceans shimmered under sunlight that pulled at their tides like a lover's call. The sun wasn't just shining—it was drinking, drawing oceans towards it, creating waves, rhythm, spin.

Everything was in motion.

Planets, moons, stars—all dancing in a massive spiral, tugging and pushing on each other. A cosmic churn. And amidst this universal whirlpool, Yasoda noticed something strangely familiar.

A white cloudy ring formed—like the swirl of curd when butter is extracted. And just like that, she remembered Krishna's love for butter. How he used to sneak into homes to steal it, how he'd get scolded, and how he'd still smile that innocent smile.

She smiled faintly, but the vision didn't stop.

She saw her village. Her home. The yard where they played. The doorway where she now stood, bent over her little boy.

And then—she saw herself, looking into Krishna's mouth.

Not from outside, but from inside.
She was inside the vision, peering into her own eyes from another realm.
The seer and the seen became one. The observer became the observed.
In the mud, in Krishna, in the universe—she found herself.

This was not just a magical vision. It was a mirror of awareness.

Here, Yasoda wanted to see—so the universe responded.

She saw everything.

The stars.
The oceans.
The mountains swirling in the skies.
Her own village. Her home.
And herself — standing there, looking into the mouth of Krishna.

Not just her son.
But the very god she had unknowingly fed, bathed, and scolded.

The center of every story. The beginning of time.
The end of all seeking.

In that moment, the world disappeared.
And the universe — the whole of it — opened wide.

But… she came back.

She returned to the physical world —
still breathing, still blinking — but shaken.
Confused. Breathless.

She had seen everything,
but she hadn't understood what she was seeing.

Because when the vision arrives before the perspective is ready, it cannot stay.

It's like pouring hot tea into a cracked cup.
It fills for a second… but then it leaks.

It's not that the truth didn't reveal itself.
It's that her *lens* wasn't wide enough to hold it.

Yasoda saw galaxies.
She saw the endless dance of creation.
The swirl of time and light.
And Krishna — at the center — still, smiling.

But she didn't see fully.

She saw the vastness of God…

but still thought of herself as someone *outside* of Him.

A mother. A human.
A small being standing in awe of something too big to hold.

But Krishna had shown her something else.

He didn't just show her the world.
He showed her that she was the world.
That there was no "inside" and "outside."
No "seer" and "seen."
No "mother" and "child."

Only being.

She didn't just witness a miracle —
She was the miracle itself. It's very surprising that she missed it.

In our lifes we go through these surprises every moment.

I want to draw you attention towards this *surprise.*

There's a story from the Mahabharata, from the dialogue known as the Yaksha Prashna.

Yudhishthira, the eldest of the Pandavas[puhn-duh-vuhz] — often called Dharmaraja[dhar-muh-RAH-juh] —
was once tested by a divine being who asked him many questions.

Among them, one stood out.

The Yaksha Prashna

One day, the Pandavas [PAAN-da-vas] were on a mission to help a poor Brahmin [BRAAH-ma-n] who had lost his arani [uh-RUH-nee] — the sacred wooden fire sticks used for Vedic rituals. They followed the trail into a thick forest, but as the day passed, they became tired and lost their way. To make things worse, they were extremely thirsty.

Yudhishthira [yu-DHISH-thi-ra], the eldest, asked Nakula [NAH-koo-la], the youngest brother, to climb a tree and look around for water.

Nakula spotted a shimmering lake not far away. He rushed toward it.

But he didn't return.

Worried, Sahadeva [sa-ha-DAY-va] followed him.

He too vanished.

Then Arjuna, the mighty archer, went.

No return.

Bhima, the strongest among them, charged ahead. Still, silence.

All four brothers — gone.

Yudhishthira now knew something was terribly wrong. He walked toward the lake and was shocked to find all his brothers lying on the ground — lifeless. Their bodies showed no wounds. No signs of struggle. Just stillness — like sleep, but colder.

As he stepped closer to the water, a voice echoed from the air:

"Do not drink until you answer my questions.

I am a Yaksha [YUK-sha].
Your brothers ignored me.
That is why they lie here dead."

Yudhishthira stood still. He didn't argue. He didn't panic.

He listened — carefully.

This was not a fight of swords. This was a test of the mind.

The Yaksha began asking questions.

Not about weapons.

Not about enemies.

But about life, death, truth, and the unseen fabric of existence.

Among all the questions the Yaksha asked, one stood out:

"What is the most surprising thing in the world?"

Yudhishthira answered:

"Day after day, people see others die.

Still, each one believes they are immortal."

This — he said — is the greatest wonder.

We witness death constantly.

In the news. In hospitals. At funeral pyres. In strangers and loved ones.

And yet… we live as if we are the exception.

We plan for years ahead. We chase status, security, and success.

We collect things, build walls, and hold grudges — all as if we'll live forever.

Death is in front of our eyes — but not inside our understanding.

We see it.

But we don't feel it.

That's the difference between seeing… and knowing.

And Yasoda was caught in that same space.

She saw a vision that should have burned away her identity. But she held on.

To her name.

To her role.
To her separate self.

She looked into Krishna's mouth,
and didn't realize what she was really looking at... was herself.

She thought she was standing in front of her son. But she was standing in front of her own reflection — cosmic, ancient, endless.

She was not outside the miracle. She was the miracle.

But the part of her that could have accepted this
was still wrapped in form.
In habit. In the comfort of being "someone."

So when the door of the universe opened,
she stepped back.

To step in,
you must let go of the one who is looking.

Only then does seeing become merging.
And merging becomes freedom.

And this is why the sages gave us the
Mahāvākya:

"**Tat Tvam Asi**" That Thou Art.

Not a lesson.

Not a concept.
A realization.

You are that.
I am that.
There is no "that" outside of you.

The dust.
The light.
The silence.
The swirl.
The God.
The gaze.
You.

You are not a watcher of truth.
You are truth, watching.

You are not someone finding the light.
You are the light that's remembering itself.

You are not outside the story.
You are the story, the page, the author, the ink.

The key is not just to see.
But to see from the right place. And that place… is within.

CHAPTER 7

I AM THAT

Sometimes, we meet someone for the first time— but they feel… familiar.
Like we've known them for years.

And other times, we meet people who instantly disturb something in us.
They haven't done anything wrong.
But something about them doesn't sit right. They feel… off.

We walk into a new home, a village, or even a temple, and it feels like we've been there before.
Though our memory says no, our body quietly says yes.

There are places that pull us, and places that reject us. Without reason.

We hear stories too— of animals attacking people for no reason…
and sometimes, animals not attacking even when they could.

It makes you wonder— what lies beneath all this?

Something unspoken moves through all this.
A quiet thread that doesn't follow logic. But it *feels real.*

And somewhere in that thread, a deep question arises:

Does the other side know me too?
Does it recognize me like I recognize it?
Is the person in front of me also feeling this invisible familiarity?
Is the place remembering me, the way I feel it in my bones?
Was I — or some part of me — present in the stories of this land, in the memory of this animal, in the silence of this stone?

That's when a soft voice inside begins to echo —
If the other person is recognizing me,
if the place is remembering me,
if the animal holds me somewhere in its memory…
then who am I really,
compared to the 'me' they are looking at?

"Am I different… or am I exactly that — which they are seeing?"
How close is it? And what might have changed?

Most of the time, we only look at the high-tempo feelings — joy, anger, love, fear.
But beneath all that, there's a slower current.

Even when we don't speak of it,

deep inside, everyone feels something about everything… every time.
Because something in us already *knows*.

Knows that everything we see is not completely "other."
Knows that difference is just one shape of sameness.
That what's looking… and what's being looked at…
is made of the same fabric.

Then the mind interrupts —
"You're just identifying with things outside yourself."
"You're being too emotional."

But this isn't imagination. It's *intimacy*.
It's what happens when you look long enough
and deep enough… that the boundary blurs.

You're not trying to become the other. You're simply realizing you were never separate to begin with.

Let's peel this further. Take something living.
A bird. A cow. A person. A tree.

It is born.
It breathes.
It feeds.
It feels.
And it dies.

It may live out its natural span,

or be taken early — by accident, by disease, or by force.

But while it lives — it passes through the same rhythms we do:
Breath. Hunger. Rest. Instinct. Memory. Fear. Feeling.

At this level, we nod and say: "It's like me."

But "I am that"? That still feels poetic.

So let's go deeper.

That being —
whether bird or human or banyan tree — is made of tissues.

Tissues are made of cells. Cells from molecules. Molecules from atoms.
Atoms from subatomic particles.

Inside every atom — a nucleus. Surrounded by space.

Now we've left the poetry behind.
We've entered *structure*

Because at this level —
everything is made of the same blueprint.

Nuclei and energy.
Electrons spinning through emptiness.
A dance of forces.
Patterns in motion.

You and the mountain — made of the same stardust. You and that cow —
running on the same electrical impulses, carrying the same oxygen built from the same hydrogen
formed inside collapsing stars.

The calcium in your bones once floated inside supernovas.
The water in your eyes has circled this Earth for millions of years —
as ocean, as cloud, as river, as tear.

Your breath may have once been in the lungs of a lion.
Or the leaf of a Bodhi tree.
Or the sigh of a monk in the Himalayas.

So now, when we say: "I am that."

We're not guessing. We're not claiming enlightenment.

We're just saying: "I looked closely. And I saw the design."

It's no longer belief. It's just what's there.

And at this point, the idea of *other* begins to melt.
The wall between "me" and "not-me" doesn't need to be broken.
It just… dissolves.

The tree and the tear. The stone and the smile. The breath and the bone. All of it —

same cloth. Just folded in different ways.

This is where separation collapses.Not because we wanted it to. But because it had nowhere else to go. There's no outside. There's no watcher and watched.

No one watching, no one being watched. Only the looking... and the looked at. And somewhere in between, a strange familiarity... a presence that feels like us.

So when we say — "I am That" it doesn't come from thought. It's not belief. It's not a philosophy. It comes from quiet recognition. Like something inside has stopped resisting, and simply recognised itself. But then — another voice rises.

"If I am That...then why do I still feel separate sometimes?"

Not from the tree.
Not from the dust.
Not from the bird.
But from the moment itself. And that's where the loop begins. Sometimes, I feel like a spectator.
Like I'm watching life from the outside. And this is the loop. The seeker's loop.

"Am I That?"
"Am I not That?"
"If I'm not That, who's asking?"
"If I am That, then why this gap?"

Here's the twist — Even the one who says "I'm not That" — is also me.
That voice, that doubt, that confusion — it's all happening within me.

So now the question isn't spiritual. It's personal.

Who am I really? The one who says "I am That"? The one who doubts it?

Or the one watching both thoughts rise and fall — silently, without needing to fix either?

And slowly, something subtle comes into view.
Maybe I'm not either side.
Maybe…
I am the space in which both arise.

To see that space —
We have to let go of both identities.
"I am That" can become another role.
"I am not That" becomes another fear.
And both keep spinning in the same circle —
endlessly defining, correcting, reacting.

The sages warned of this.
They called it the trap of duality —
where truth becomes a mental fight,
and presence becomes a back-and-forth match

between the self we know and the self we seek.

And in that game,
truth slips away.

So the rishis said —
Don't pick a side.
Go beyond both.

Beyond *yes* and *no*.
Beyond *this* and *that*.
Beyond even the voice that says "go beyond."

Rest in the space
where everything is allowed to exist
but nothing clings.

That space is not a goal.
Not a title.
Not even a state.

That space is **Turiya** — The 4th Dimension.
Not physical.
Not mental.
Not even the dream world.

It is the undercurrent behind all three.

The silent layer beneath waking, dreaming, and deep sleep.
The unseen screen on which all life plays.

Turiya is not something we "attain."
It's what remains
when all effort to become
finally… stops.

CHAPTER 8

TURIYA THE 4TH DIMENSION

When we start seeing — not with effort, not with force, but with a relaxed, clear attention — something unusual begins to happen.

Not brighter colours.
Not sudden wisdom. But sound.
Not the sound from footsteps, or words, or even breath.
This is a quieter sound. It doesn't come through the ears.
It comes from somewhere… **behind the eyes**.

It feels like the silence itself is speaking. But it doesn't use words.
And strangely — it feels like… **us**.

Not the "me" looking at the world —
but the "me" inside the world I'm looking at.

That's when the wall between seer and seen begins to melt.
We are not just looking at the world.
We are inside it.
And it… is inside us.

The more we soften,
the more we stop dividing —
the more we notice:

Thoughts no longer arrive from memory or noise.
They rise like whispers from within the thing we are observing.
It's not borrowed truth. It's not second-hand wisdom. It's our own truth.
Shaped by how we see,
by how we've lived,
by how we are here now.

And slowly, we don't just watch what we're looking at —
we start becoming it.

Let's take a simple example.

Have you ever sat in a dark theatre, watching a movie?

For a while, you forget where you are.
You get pulled into the story — the character becomes you.

You laugh when they laugh. You cry when they cry.
For that moment, you are not watching a film — **you are inside it.**

But… when the movie ends, you step outside.
You return to being "you" again.
The same person, now remembering the whole story like a dream.

What if someone asked,

"Who were you really — the person in the seat, or the one inside the movie?"

We stop feeling like we're separate.
We begin to feel like we're becoming what we see.
Or rather… it is becoming us.

But then… a question rises.

Who is this "me" who is seeing and becoming?

To understand this, let's step into a story.

King Janaka's Dream

King Janaka [JAH-nuh-kuh] was one of the wisest kings of ancient India.

One afternoon, after a long morning and a full meal, he lay down to rest.

And as he drifted into sleep, he dreamed.

In his dream, enemies attacked his kingdom.

His soldiers fell.

His palace was burning.

He ran for his life into the forest.

Wounded. Hungry. Lost.

He wandered alone for days.

Finally, a kind old woman let him stay in her hut.

She had some rice and lentils.

But her hands were too weak to cook.

She said, "Son, if you're hungry, you must prepare it."

Janaka agreed. He cooked the food.

The smell made his stomach growl.

He placed it on two plates.

But just as he lifted his first bite —

a dog leapt into the hut,

grabbed the plate, and ran.

Janaka cried out — and in that cry, he woke up.

He was in his bed.

Soft silk. Cool air. Servants nearby.

Everything was calm. Everything was fine.

But one question haunted him:

"Was I a beggar in the forest… or am I a king now?"

He asked his ministers.

His sages.

His wise men.

But none could satisfy him.

Because this was not a question of facts —
it was a crack in his *sense of self.*

Then a boy entered the court. Bent in eight places. Calm. Luminous. He walked slowly, but his presence filled the hall.

Ashtavakra [ASH-ta-vuh-kra].

Barely a teenager, yet known across kingdoms for his unmatched wisdom.
Born with a deformed body, but a mind untouched by confusion.
He spoke not from books — but from the direct seeing of truth.
And what he saw became the **Ashtavakra Gita** —

a deep, bold conversation between him and Janaka himself. A text that doesn't explain the world — it strips it away.

Janaka looked at him and asked,

"**Am I the beggar... or the king**?"

Ashtavakra smiled gently and said:

"You are neither the beggar nor the king.

You are the one who saw the beggar.

You are the one who sees the king.

You are that awareness behind both.

You are that which never changes —

while all else comes and goes."

This is what the sages called **Turiya** [too-REE-yah]. The Fourth.

Not waking.
Not dreaming.
Not deep sleep.
But that in-between

where all three arise and dissolve.
The background of all experience.
The watcher behind all seeing.

Turiya

Not another version of yourself.
But the space where all versions appear.
Not a dreamer. Not the dream.
But the one who sees both.

The quiet witness.
The presence that is not touched by dreams, or sleep, or even wakefulness.

Mandukya Upanishad says it like this

Mandukya Upanishad – Mantra 7:

Nāntaḥ-prajñam na bahiṣ-prajñam nobhayataḥ-prajñam na prajñāna-ghanam na prajñam nāprajñam	न अन्तःप्रज्ञं न बहिःप्रज्ञं न उभयतःप्रज्ञं न प्रज्ञानघनं न प्रज्ञं न अप्रज्ञम्।
adṛṣṭam avyavahāryam	अदृष्टम् अव्यवहार्यम्
agrāhyam alakṣaṇam	अग्राह्यम् अलक्षणम्
acintyam avyapadeśyam	अचिन्त्यम् अव्यपदेश्यम्
ekātma-pratyaya-sāram	एकात्मप्रत्ययसारम्
prapañcopaśamam śāntam śivam advaitam	प्रपञ्चोपशमम् शान्तम् शिवम् अद्वैतम्
caturtham manyante sa ātmā sa vijñeyaḥ ||	चतुर्थं मन्यन्ते स आत्मा स विज्ञेयः॥

It is not what we know inside.
Not what we know outside.
Not what we think is knowledge, nor absence of it.

Not knowing, not unknowing.
It is beyond everything — and yet it holds all of it.

It is unseen, beyond interaction, incomprehensible, featureless, unthinkable, and indescribable.

It is the essence of the self that knows itself as one.
That one is **Turiya**.

The one who stays… no matter what appears.
Turiya is not something to get.
It's what's already there — when you stop trying to be anything else.

It is not "I am That."
It is not "I am not That."
It is **the space where both rise and fall** — like *waves in the ocean.*

It is not a state. It is a dimension.
The background of every thought, role, form, and name.

You've probably had moments where you're awake — but don't feel awake.
Moments when you're in a dream — but you feel someone is watching you.

Moments in silence — when everything inside you is still… but something is still listening.

That is, it. That's the witness. That's the space behind the noise. That's the part of you that sees without becoming what it sees. It is not cold. It is not distant.

It is simply still. And when you rest in that stillness, you're no longer trying to prove anything.
You're no longer trying to fix or chase. You just see.

And in that seeing, something unexpected begins to happen:
You don't just witness the world.
You create it

I Create, Therefore I Am.

Because the one who sees purely — starts to shape reality without effort. And that is where the next doorway opens…

CHAPTER 9

I CREATE, THEREFORE I AM

Once we begin to see clearly, and hear what silence is saying, something else begins to reveal itself. Creation, not the kind where we build things with our hands — but the kind that happens quietly… just because we're here.

We begin to realise:
The world isn't just something we walk into. It's something we keep projecting — moment after moment.

We're not entering reality. We're shaping it as we go.

Every word we speak,
every thought we carry,
every wound we haven't healed —
acts like colour on a brush.
And what we call "the world"

is the painting we never knew we were painting.

The world isn't just happening to us. We are happening to the world. That's why I say:
I create, therefore I am. There's a powerful illusion at play. We often believe what we see is truth a fixed reality that exists on its own.

But look again.

Two people walk into the same room.
One feels warmth.
One feels judged.
The room didn't change — but their world wasn't the same.

Because their creation wasn't the same.

We don't just perceive the world. We project it.

And that projection is shaped by who we are in that moment —

our emotion, our memory, our hunger, our longing.

Let's imagine a mirror.

When you stand before it, the reflection appears. But if *you're* not there, the mirror reflects nothing. It doesn't store an image of the past, nor does it imagine your future. It only reflects what you bring into its presence.

The same is true for the world.

It reflects you.

The sky doesn't carry meaning.

The tree doesn't call itself beautiful.

The wind doesn't whisper anything in particular.

We do.

We are the ones who give names,

who place value,

who paint emotion into everything we *see.*

That's creation.

Now imagine this:

Each night, we fall asleep —

and we dream.

In that dream, we create people,

places, sounds, danger, love, time, even pain.

And it all feels so real — until we wake up.

Then everything vanishes.

But here's the question:

If we can create a full reality while asleep…

what makes us so sure this waking world isn't also a dream?

Just a more stable one. Just a longer one. What if this is also a projection?

The great sages knew this. They didn't just say, "I think, therefore I am."

They said, "I project, therefore I become." "I create, therefore I am."

It is not enough to observe. It is not enough to know. It is when you realize that you are the cause, not the effect, that true *seeing* begins.

Even silence is a kind of creation. You may sit quietly in nature. You hear the birds, feel the breeze. But something more is happening. Something subtle.

You're not just receiving the moment. You're **creating** it—by the way you receive it.
Your *attention* gives the breeze its poetry.
Your *presence* gives the bird its song.
Your *stillness* gives the trees their depth.

The world becomes meaningful **because you are here**.

Not as a guest. But as the **source**.

Everything you experience—whether it comes through the eyes, ears, skin, or thought—is being shaped by your own internal field. Like a projector casting a film onto a blank screen, your inner state determines what story unfolds.

And yet, we rarely pause to ask:

"Who is the projector?"

"What film is being played?"

"And who wrote the script?"

The answer to all of them is the same: **I did**.

I wrote the script.
I built the projector.
I chose the lens.
I cast the light.

I am not a character in the play.
I am the one who created the play

So, what happens when I stop playing the role and start becoming the creator?

Everything shifts. This is the beginning of *responsibility*—not the heavy kind, but the luminous kind. When you know that you are the creator, then your suffering is not punishment. It's a *reflection*. And your joy is not luck. It's a *signal*. Whatever is happening outside is pointing to what's happening within.

The outer world becomes your personal scripture, speaking in symbols that only you can read.Because it is written in your language. Because it is made from yourself.

So, when I say, "I create, therefore I am," it is not arrogance.
It is truth.
It is not separation.
It is union.

It is not about controlling the world. It is about *recognizing*: There is no world apart from me.

But even that recognition asks for something quiet, something often forgotten— An eye that can listen.

Because not everything we create is loud. Some truths don't appear in *sight*. They arrive… in soundless sound. In the space between thoughts. In the silence behind a bird's wings. In the feeling we can't name but still understand. And if we listen closely— if we develop not just vision, but that inner hearing…

That's where the next chapter begins.

Not with the eye that sees.

But with the eye that listens.

CHAPTER 10

THE EYE THAT LISTENS

We think we see with our eyes. Light enters. Shapes appear. And we call it seeing.
That's what we've been told.

But when we start paying closer attention, and look a little deeper…we begin to notice something else is going on. Every time we see something, something else quietly joins the moment:

A voice.

Not a sound in the air.
Not someone whispering behind us.
But a voice—inside us.
Soft. Immediate. Familiar.
It doesn't ask for permission.

It just speaks.
Sometimes it says something small.
Sometimes it says something sharp.
Sometimes it's not even words—just a knowing,
like a quick judgment that already feels true
before we even know why.

Take a simple moment.

We saw someone on the street, sitting quietly.
And without thinking, we heard:

"*Probably poor. Maybe even drunk.*"

We met someone new. They smiled. Dressed well. Confident.

And the voice said:

"*Arrogant. Fake.*"

We didn't choose these thoughts. We didn't even *notice* them most of the time.
They came from somewhere deeper. Older.

Memory, maybe. Or fear. Something absorbed. Repeated.
Not ours, but inherited— from family, society, stories, culture…
Years and years of voices layered over us like dust on a mirror.

And then one day—something in us watches that voice. Not judging it. Not suppressing it.

Just… *watching* it.

And in that watching, a space opens. A pause.

And we begin to ask:
Who's speaking?
Where does this voice come from?
And who is listening to it?

We look for the source, but it keeps shifting. We dig into the memory, and find more layers.
And more. And more. Each one feels final—until we peel it again.
And slowly, something becomes clear:
This voice is not *us*.
It's just commentary.
Refined. Repeated. Rehearsed.

But deeper than that voice, beneath all the noise,
there is another presence.

Not loud. Not reactive. It doesn't comment. It only *knows*.
Like it's been watching for lifetimes.

We've all felt it. Not just in stillness. Not just in surrender.
But in those moments when life gets *too much*.
When sorrow becomes heavy.
When joy becomes overwhelming.
When something in us breaks—

or bursts open—so wide,
that nothing outside feels like it can hold us anymore.
That's when we reach for something else.
Something quiet.
Something familiar, but wordless.
Something we've never been taught… but somehow *know*.
It's the space we try to return to
when pain is unbearable.
When confusion is loud.
When even our own thoughts feel like strangers.
We separate from people.
From voices.
From light, sometimes.
And then… we try to separate from the noise inside.
Because something inside us knows—
that only in that silence,
something true might speak.

We all search for that space. Not because we read it in a book. But because it's *built into us*.
Like firmware.

The way a newborn calf knows to reach for its mother's milk.
No one teaches it.
It simply *knows*. It's coded into its being.

And just like that— when things get too loud outside or inside— we all reach for this silent space. We try, without knowing why, to quiet everything else…
so *this* can speak. This is where our God Particle lives.

THE SCIENCE OF SILENCE

In physics, the "God Particle" is another name for the **Higgs boson**—
a tiny, elusive particle discovered after decades of searching.

What does it do?

It gives *mass* to matter.
It allows particles that would otherwise be weightless to *exist* in form.
Without it, everything would remain light, formless, drifting.
With it, things begin to *become.*

It doesn't make noise. It doesn't shine.
But it creates the field that makes reality possible.

It's everywhere.
And yet… almost impossible to detect.
Until you slow things down.
Until you strip everything else away.

That's what lives inside us, too.

A subtle field.
A silence
A sacred intelligence.
A core that gives that gives shape to our experience..

Without it, we remain scattered.
We react, we fear, we forget.

But with it—
we *return*.
We remember.
We stand.

We don't control it.
We don't summon it.
We *return* to it.

Like gravity.
Like breath.

And when we do, we don't get answers. We don't get words.
We get *knowing*.

A kind that doesn't come from thinking— but from *being*.

That's the voice behind the voice.
That's the presence beneath the noise.
That's our center.
Our witness.
Our Self.

That's our inner Higgs field.
Our invisible gravity.
The God Particle of consciousness.

That's Krishna in us. That's the Ātma.

And when we touch it—
we don't get answers.
We get *clarity*.
Not through thinking.
But through stillness.

Not by adding.
But by listening.

Even in the Mahābhārata, this truth is quietly shown.

Arjuna wasn't confused because of the war.
He was confused because of the *voices* inside him.

His heart was torn.
His mind was loud.
He saw teachers and enemies in the same glance.
He didn't trust what he saw—because he couldn't trust the one who was *seeing*.

So what did he do?

He sat.
He stepped back.

He let the noise surface.
And he waited.

And from *that* silence, Krishna spoke.
Not just as an advisor on a chariot—
but as the eternal presence *within*.

Not from outside.
But from Arjuna's *center*.
From the witness that had seen everything…
and waited without judgment.

That's Krishna.
That's the Ātma.
That's the God Particle of awareness.
And when Arjuna listened— really listened—

And in that pause — in that deep listening —
Arjuna's vision changed.
Not just his decision to fight.
But how he saw everything around him.
That's the difference.

Real clarity doesn't come from looking harder.
It comes from listening deeper.

That's what this chapter is about.
The eye behind the eyes.
The one that listens before it sees.

And when we slow down enough,
we begin to feel where that listening is coming from.
Not the brain.
Not from old memories.
Not from excitement or fear.

It felt older than all of that.
It felt like something inside us that simply knows.
Calm. Still. Wise.
It didn't say much. But when it did, it felt like truth.

Not a truth we had to think about.
Just a quiet feeling of "I am That."

Not pride. Not confusion. Just knowing.

That's the Ātma.
The one within.
Who watches without judgment.
Who listens before words.
Who sees…; even when our eyes don't.

But then came another discovery.

We couldn't always hear that voice.

There were days—long ones—when it seemed to vanish.
Not because it ran away.
But because life got too loud.

Sometimes, it was pain.
That thick, heavy kind of pain.
Where something inside us breaks and keeps breaking.
Where even silence turns into noise.

And sometimes…
it wasn't pain at all.
It was joy.
Big, bursting joy.
The kind that makes us laugh until we forget the world.
The kind that lifts us so high…
we forget we're standing on something.

Both pain and joy—
pulled us outside ourselves.

And in those moments,
that voice—our voice—grew quiet.
It didn't disappear.

It just couldn't be heard through all the feeling.

Like someone whispering during a storm.

And only when the noise settles,
when we sit still
with no agenda,
no chasing,
no running…

That's when it returns.
That same soft voice.
Not emotional.
Not dramatic.
Just there.
Like it had always been.

And when it returns—
our eyes see differently.

Not just shapes.
Not just names.
But meaning.

We don't just look at the tree—
we feel its *patience*.

We don't just glance at the sky—
we hear its *distance*.

We don't just meet someone—
we sense their *longing*.

Because the real eye...
is the one that listens first.

That's why the rishis spoke of the third eye—
not just as a mystical center—
but as a *listening* space.

An eye that listens before it judges.
An eye that waits before it names.
An eye that receives before it reflects.

And in that listening—
the whole field becomes clear.

So now, we understand:
We create the world.
But first—
we must *listen* to it.
And when we listen deeply,
we don't just hear truth.
We become the space in which truth becomes clear.

The Clarity That Sees

CHAPTER 11

THE CLARITY THAT SEES

After the listening… we don't immediately see something dramatic. What we hear doesn't always give us instant answers. It gives us something softer—presence.

But if we stay with it long enough… something inside begins to shift.

It's hard to explain. At first, nothing changes outside. But something in how we're seeing begins to settle. We notice we're not in a rush to understand. We're just… present. And in that presence, something starts to form—clarity.

But this clarity doesn't come fast. It doesn't arrive just because we heard something true. It begins only when we're willing to keep looking—without forcing a conclusion. We've started to realize:

Clarity is not a spotlight. It's a space. A space we must sit in. A space we must allow to open in its own time. We can't drag it open. We can only stay still and let it unfold. This is where Kāl [kaal] enters. Not as a clock on the wall— but as that unseen hand that ripens truth inside us.

Like fruit falling when it's Mature/ Paripakv [puh-ree-puhk-vuh] (परिपाक)— clarity comes when we are ready to hold it.

The Upanishads says:

तस्य भासाऽ सर्वम् इदं विभाति।

"Tasya bhāsā sarvam idam vibhāti."

— By Its light, all this shines.

But that Light… doesn't come when we snap our fingers. It doesn't respond to rituals, noise, or bargains. It's not summoned — it's uncovered.

Like the **Turiya** state described in the **Mandukya Upanishad**,
this Light is not something we see outside or inside.
Not a dream, not a thought, not even a deep silence.
It is not **prajñā** — not knowledge.
Not **aprajñā** — not ignorance.
It is beyond.
Yet it is the very ground on which all states rest.

Unseeable. Untouchable. Unimaginable.
And yet — more real than all we think we are.

To reach it, we don't climb upward. We don't achieve it like a goal.
We **shed**. Layer by layer.

Mask by mask. Belief by belief

And this is the realm of **Mahākāl** [muh-haa-kaal] — the Great Time, Not just the time on clocks,

but the timeless One who lives in the background of every change.
He is not a destroyer of life. He is a dissolver of illusion.

Mahākāl doesn't give us the truth in a gift box.
He takes away what is not truth —

Sometimes slowly.
Sometimes painfully.
Always with purpose.

He dissolves our identities.
He burns the false beliefs we keep holding on to —
He silences the loud voice in our head until
we begin to hear… not sound, but Source. Not information.
But clarity.

Until the one who was looking disappears,
and all that remains is the seeing itself.

No drama. No achievement. Just **Being** — simple, silent, and sovereign.

This is not a Light we can light. It is the Light that lights all lights.
And Mahākāl is the sacred darkness that guards it.

He doesn't rush. He doesn't comfort.
He only removes — until there is nothing left to hide. Nothing left to protect.

And then… what shines, shines by Itself. And when that clarity arrives,
it's not loud. It doesn't come with fireworks. It comes as a **mood**.

Not happy or sad. But quiet. Clean. Spacious.

Like a cool wind that says, "You don't need to chase anymore."
And everything changes.
Not outside. But in how we see. We stop reacting. Our energy softens. The world stops looking like a battle.

Even our words feel different. Because they're not coming from confusion. They're coming from stillness.

And that stillness— creates the world around us.

We used to think:
The world shapes our thoughts.

Now we see:
Our clarity shapes our moods.
Our moods shape our actions.
Our actions shape the world we walk through.

The shift is not "out there."
The shift is in how we're looking.

And how we look—depends on one thing:
Intention. Not ambition.
Not wanting to be "right."

But the pure desire: To see what's true. Even if it dissolves us.

We remembered **Yasoda** again.

She did look deeply.
She saw the entire universe inside Krishna's mouth. Not just planets and stars—
She saw her home. Her village. Herself…standing there looking inside Krishna.

For a moment—just a moment— she was standing at the top of the mountain. The view was total. The Truth was open. But her intention was still small. She was still asking: "Did he eat mud?"

So she saw everything— but missed what it meant. She had the **vision**…but not the **clarity to stay.**

Because she didn't surrender.

The *Garuda Purana* tells a similar tale.
Once, the great sage Vishnu Sharma was asked:
"How do we reach the highest truth?"

And he said:
"You cannot hold truth like a fruit.
You must become the tree...
and let truth land when it wants."

That's what Yasoda missed.
She saw it. But she couldn't become empty enough to stay in it. And so the vision left. And we began to understand:

Going deep is not enough.
Seeing truth is not enough.

To remain with it—
we must surrender. Surrender not just our ignorance, but even our curiosity. Even the hunger for answers.

Because real clarity doesn't reward *cleverness*. It doesn't bloom under *restlessness*. It doesn't shine for the one who wants to know.

It appears...only when the one who wants disappears. Not escape— but union.

When we give time—Kāl— and stay with that pure intention, Mahākāl begins His quiet work. And if we stay just a little longer, clarity becomes a doorway

But that doorway doesn't lead to more knowing. It leads to *un-becoming.*

Not destruction.
Not silence.
But something gentler.
Something more complete.

We begin to enter the space that holds everything and yet, is not anything.

This is what the sages pointed to. The great emptiness that is not lack but wholeness.
Not absence but totality. They called it:
Mahā Shūnya [muh-haa shoon-yah]**.**
The Great Nothing.

The place where the seer dissolves…and only the seeing remains.
Where the one who once chased everything
becomes nothing—
and in that, becomes *everything.*

Nothing, the Final Everything.

So if you're holding a little clarity now—

don't rush to use it.
Don't try to teach it.
Don't even try to explain it.

Just sit.
Let it burn softly through your sight.
Let it un-name what you thought you were.

Because what is true…
opens only when you stop chasing it.
And when you stop being the seeker—the truth begins to see through *you*.

CHAPTER 12

NOTHING, THE FINAL EVERYTHING.

So, all this while, we've come to understand one simple thing:
When clarity begins to rise in us, it doesn't feel like a fact.
It feels like a mood. A mood so clean and quiet… that we stop chasing life.
We begin watching it.

And that watching— slowly, silently— starts to become understanding.
But this understanding doesn't arrive all at once.
It's not a flash. It's a deep, soft unfolding.
It comes only when we wait. When we don't rush.

When we let **Kāl**—Time itself—do his work.

Because Mahākāl is not a fast teacher.

He doesn't explain.
He doesn't shout.
He doesn't reward urgency.
He just keeps peeling away everything that's not true,
layer by layer... until only truth remains. And that final layer?
It's not something. It's nothing.

Let me say it clearly:

The only thing that truly exists... is nothingness.

Not emptiness like a blank wall.
Not blankness. Not silence like a room with no sound.

But a space where all false things have fallen—

and what's left is real, alive, untouched.

That's what the sages called **Mahā Shūnya** the Great Nothing.

Not an absence, but a return.
Not an escape, but the end of illusion.

And in my view:

To reach Mahā Shūnya, there are only two real paths—

1. Let Go.
2. Know Fully.

1. Let Go.

Let go of control.
Let go of labels.
Let go of trying to be someone.

Let **Mahākāl** do what He does best.
Let Him show you that your identity—
your name, your stories, your roles—
were only shadows on a screen.

And when you stop trying to hold the light—
you fall into it.

2. Know Fully.

Keep looking.
Keep asking.
Keep learning—
until even the one who *knows* disappears.

Go so deep into the sound, the vision, the meaning—
that you reach the place where meaning ends.

And something strange happens there:

Infinity becomes zero.
And zero becomes infinity.

There's no difference anymore.
No separation between all and nothing.

Like the quiet truth behind all equations:

$$\infty - \infty = \infty$$

You take everything away— and still, what remains is everything.

You become the full… by becoming the empty.

That's why the Vedas say:

Om Pūr*ṇ*am ada*ḥ*, pūr*ṇ*am idam,Pūr*ṇ*āt pūr*ṇ*am udacyate. Pūr*ṇ*asya pūr*ṇ*am ādāya, Pūr*ṇ*am evāvaśiṣyate.	ॐ पूर्णमदः पूर्णमिदं पूर्णात् पूर्णमुदच्यते। पूर्णस्य पूर्णमादाय पूर्णमेवावशिष्यते॥

That is full. This is full.
From fullness arises fullness.
Even when fullness is taken from fullness—
what remains is still fullness.

Nothing lost. Nothing broken. Nothing ever missing.

I am nothing.

And in that… I become free.

Free from time.
Free from story.

Free from self.

This is not death. This is freedom— from everything that ever pretended to be *me*. We all get glimpses of this space. In silence. In surrender. In the kind of clarity that comes without any reason.

The only real question is: Will we stay long enough to touch it? Because once you touch **Mahā Shūnya**... Once it touches *you*... you don't just see the truth. **You *become* the truth.**

CHAPTER 13

TRUTH: YOU ARE THE DISTRACTION YOU DIED CHASING

Truth is not just one thing. It doesn't wear just one name or walk only one path. It doesn't rise from only one scripture, and it doesn't belong to any one person.

It comes in many forms.

In silence. In sound.

In logic. In madness.

In birth… and also in death.

Sometimes it arrives as light.
Sometimes it hides behind a shadow.
Sometimes it holds your hand.
Sometimes it burns everything you love.

And still— we keep calling it truth. We keep chasing it.

There are those who hold on too tightly— to what they think is right.
To what they think is sacred. To their version of the world, their roles, their meanings.

And so, they stay in the cycle.
Janma. Mrityu. Punarjanma.

- **Janma** [JAN-muh] - *Birth*
- **Mrityu** [MRIT-yoo]- *Death*
- **Punarjanma**[POO-nar-JAN-muh]- *Rebirth*

Truth comes to them again and again. But they see it only in parts.

Like reading one line of a poem and thinking you know the whole story. Time becomes their teacher. And Mahakal is a slow teacher. So they keep moving in loops. From life to life. From question to question.

But some begin to loosen their grip. They stop asking "What is truth?" And instead, they ask "Who is asking?" They stop collecting answers. They begin to witness. They watch the dance of Satyam [SUT-yum] /truth.

They see how truth destroys. They see how it heals.
They see how it dances as beauty… and disappears again.
And in watching that… something inside breaks open.

They stop needing truth to be fixed.
They stop holding it like a sword. They wear it lightly—
like **vibhuti** [vi-BHOO-tee] on the forehead. Just a reminder: Everything burns. And that's okay.

They surrender to the dance— The dance of **Satyam**, the truth that never stands still.
The fire of **Shivam**, which burns everything that's false. And slowly… slowly…
a rhythm awakens inside them.

They no longer say,
"This is happening to me." They begin to feel—
"This is happening *as* me."

And then… they don't run after beauty anymore. They become it.

Not the beauty of a face. Not the beauty of a flower.
But the beauty of the one who is no longer chasing.

That beauty has a name: **Sundaram** [SOON-duh-rum]. Because it is born when **truth has finished dancing**, and the self has stopped clinging.

Think of the one who watches all the shades of truth without grabbing any of them.

That one doesn't fight **Shivam's fire.**
That one doesn't cling to **Satyam's rhythm.**
That one opens their arms and lets it all pass through.
That is not weakness.
That is not surrender.

That is the poison turned to nectar.
That is halāhala becoming amṛta.

That is the moment when truth softens…
and *you* become still.

You're no longer holding onto reality.
You're letting it pass through you—

like wind.
Like fire.
Like time.

Like **Shiva** sitting in the cremation ground, you no longer run from endings.
You hold them gently— until they become beginnings again.

And in that place… you don't need truth anymore. Because the one who *needed* truth—
is also gone.

What remains?

Nothing you can name.
Nothing you can write.
Nothing you can hold up and say, "This is it."

Because whatever can be held— will be burned.
Whatever can be spoken— will dissolve.
Whatever can be known—is still within the dance.

Only **Satyam** remains—
the truth that dances through form,
through beauty,
through destruction,
through desire.
It moves like fire moves through wood—
lighting, consuming, disappearing.

Satyam is that dance. And most of us are trapped in it— in the rhythm of meaning-making.

In the hope that we'll catch truth if we move fast enough. But truth dances faster. So we keep spinning.

But then… something happens. The spinning slows. The questions lose their teeth.
And we begin to see— **Shivam**.

Shivam. The stillness. The presence that never chased, never changed, never flinched.

Shivam is the flame after the burn. What stays when there is nothing left to seek.

Like the Kathopanishad [Kuh-THO-puh-ni-shud] says:

Yada sarve pramucyante kāmā ye'sya hṛdi śritāḥ, atha martyo'mṛto bhavati — atra brahma samāśnute.	यदा सर्वे प्रमुच्यन्ते कामा येऽस्य हृदि श्रिताः। अथ मर्त्योऽमृतो भवत्यत्र ब्रह्म समश्नुते ॥

"When all desires dwelling in the heart fall away,
the mortal becomes immortal— and here, in this very life, he realizes Brahman."

That *dropping* of desire… is Shivam.
Not a concept. A condition.
A state where the dance ends

and only watching remains.

And from that stillness—

emerges something unexplainable.

Not truth. Not silence. Not bliss.

Something else.
Something *after* the end.

Everyone says,
"Shiva is the Sundar."
The beautiful one. The ultimate aesthetic.

But I've always wondered— are they talking about **Shiva**… or are they mistaking **Sundaram** for something Shiva *causes*? To me, **Sundaram** is not a description. It's not a trait. It's not how Shiva *looks*.

Sundaram is not beauty you see.
It is beauty that happens.

Sundaram is not a thing. It is a moment. An event. A becoming.

It's the *after*. The residue. The hush after everything has been burned,
and nothing else moves.

It is what's left when you've chased truth
so completely,

so obsessively,
that there is no more space left inside you to move.

And you fall— not down… but inward.

You become **Nishchala**.
Motionless. Still… like the center of a flame.

And that's when something begins—
something beyond your effort,
beyond your seeking,
beyond even your surrender.

You don't find Shiva.
You don't reach him.
He… reaches *you*.

Not with fire,
not with thunder,
but with something softer.
Something wordless.

And **in that moment**,
without warning,
without you even realizing it— That event is **Sundaram.**

That final shimmer of you
just before you disappear.

That beauty that glows

because it's about to vanish.

That last trace of separation
which is so tender, so luminous,
that Shiva Himself stops
—to embrace it.

You are that Sundaram.
In *Satyam Shivam Sundaram*,
Sundaram is you.

Every Ātman turns beautiful
before it merges with the eternal.
That beauty isn't in Shiva.
It's in you—
as you become Him.

A quiet, unspeakable becoming that doesn't want to be explained. It just wants to be held.

So yes—
Whoever truly chases **Satyam**,
inevitably reaches **Shivam**.
And the one who surrenders into that stillness…
undergoes the most beautiful becoming of all.

They don't find truth.
They don't touch God.
They **become** the silence that God never left.

And *that* is the secret of **Sundaram**.

"Nishchala tattvam Shivam uchyate"
– *That which is unmoving… is called Shiva.*

And now we see it clearly—
Truth itself was the distraction.
The most seductive one.
The most convincing lie.

Because as long as there is a seeker,
there will always be something to seek.
As long as there is a "you" who chases truth,
there will always be one more step… one more question…
one more dance.

But the chase doesn't end when the answer arrives.
It ends when the one who's chasing
can no longer hold the chase.

The distraction ends
when **you** end—
not your body, not your breath—
but the part of you that was always trying to become something.

Because when the search for **Satya** is followed all the way,
it doesn't lead to more knowledge.
It leads to **Moksha**.

And **Moksha** isn't a destination.
It isn't heaven.
It isn't bliss.

It is **becoming the source**.
The drop dissolving back into the ocean.
The dancer vanishing into the silence that was always there.

But for that to happen—
the creation must die.

You can't carry your name
and merge into the nameless.
You can't hold the flame
and become the light.

The **dance must stop.**
The **dancer must disappear.**

And in that disappearance…

Sundaram happens.

The beauty that doesn't shout.
The stillness that doesn't move.
The truth that doesn't need to be known—
because it already *is*.

So what remains?

Nothing you can hold.

Nothing you can explain.
Nothing you can become.

Only…

what you always were
before the seeking began.
The silence before the dance.
The space behind the name.
The truth before the truth.

Truth = You Are the Distraction You Died Chasing.

And only in dying that death… does real life begin.

AFTERMATH: THE SILENCE THAT WATCHES

Now that you've read it all,

don't rush to understand.

Let it sit.

Let it echo.

Let it sting, soften, or slip away.

Because this isn't a truth to be remembered.

It's a rhythm to be forgotten into.

You don't have to hold on to any of it.

In fact, you're not supposed to.

If something inside you has loosened–

even a little–

then the book is already over.

There is nothing more to find.

Nothing more to fix.

Just this:

Let it burn what needs to burn.

Let it bloom what needs to bloom.

And if one day,

you find yourself no longer chasing...

no longer naming...

just watching—

then know this:

That watcher was always there.

It just waited for you to get out of the way.

A QUIET INVITATION

If something in this book touched you—

not just as a thought,

but like a breath...

or a scar...

or a strange kind of freedom—

write to it.

Whisper back.

Even if it's just one line.

Not to me.

To **yourself.**

Or pass this book to someone who's still spinning.

Someone still dancing.

Someone still dying to be still.

Not to change them.

Not to save them.

Just to remind them:

They were never the one who needed saving.

To Continue The Dialogue Beyond These Pages—

Website: www.vjbharath.com

Instagram: @vjbharathbooks

X (Twitter): @VJBharathReddy